LEGENDARY LEADERSHIP

LEGENDARY LEADERSHIP

HOW ORDINARY PEOPLE BECOME UNCOMMON LEADERS

DR. BRUCE B. BAIRD

MUSE
LITERARY

Muse Literary

TABLE OF CONTENTS

PREFACE

One of the biggest worries I had when I first considered a title for the book you're holding in your hands, is that any one of a good number of former employees might see the book, do a double-take when they saw my photo on the back cover of a book titled *Legendary Leadership*, rub their eyes to make sure they were seeing straight, and be utterly confused or laughably entertained that by some unaccountable miracle I had transformed into someone who actually had something to say about leadership.

I must say I can't fault any of those early employees for thinking this way. At one time or another, I think everybody in Granbury, Texas, used to work for me. They used to come and go so fast my head would spin. I'd like to think that I would be the first to admit I was the worst boss in the world, but I'm pretty sure some of those early hires would beat me to the punch.

So, what happened? I'll address this at greater length in the pages ahead, but suffice it to say that I learned a lot over the years—about myself, about others, and about running productive businesses.

But learning doesn't always come easily. Among other things, it requires mistakes and loss and downright failure; it requires help from mentors along the way; and above all, it requires reflection.

I know what you're thinking. "Okay, Bruce. But still. You went from the *Worst Boss In The World to Legendary*? As in Fabled? Heroic? In one lifetime?

Fair enough. But my point is not so much to present myself as a legendary leader, as it is to encourage you to have legendary leadership as something to strive for, a goal—to have that holy grail of legendary leadership hovering out there in front of you as a symbol of aspiration, something to work toward in every interaction, every relationship, in every minute of every day. There is no such thing as arrival at the doorstep of leadership. Though I've made great strides in leadership since those early days, I'm constantly learning new ways to be a better leader.

I made some pretty epic mistakes along the way, too, but the failures and losses are every bit as responsible for growth and development as the victories. The fact that you're reading this introduction is an indication that you are interested in your own development as a leader, and my hope is that something in this book helps you in that regard—that something here stays with you and helps bring you a bit closer to the title on the cover.

WHAT WE TALK ABOUT WHEN WE TALK ABOUT REFLECTION

Chapter 1

WHAT IT MEANS TO BE A LEGENDARY LEADER

I like the idea of you starting off this journey with me from a strong position. Starting off on the right foot was a goal of mine even in my bad-boss days. How's this for starters: you can't possibly be a worse leader than I was at the start. You'll hear a story or two about those days in every chapter of this book, but I'll start by looking a little closer at one of the traits I mentioned in the introduction as a paramount element of leadership—the conscious decision to reflect.

I have often been asked what it was that could be credited with my journey from bad boss to where I am today—which is, inarguably, a much better place. Was it a core value shift that took place? Was it some epic failure or loss that was placed in my path to wake me up? Is there a single incident I could trace the shift back to?

I can't say there were any Road to Damascus experiences that I can credit with radically changing everything. There are a couple of less epic stories that played a part, but, more than anything, it was a greater openness to self-reflection that took place somewhere along the way. I have always thought about myself as a reflective person, but more and more I realize that I was selectively reflective.

One of the things I've always had going for me is that I'm a hard worker. From an early age, I always had a knack for making money. There was never a time in my life that I worried I wouldn't be able to make money. My early experiences with self-reflection were limited to reflecting on the joy of making money, and reflecting on how I could make more of it.

My first business got off the ground when I was nine years old. I started a neighborhood newspaper with a printing press I received as a Christmas gift. I used it to put out information about what the kids were up to in the neighborhood. I put out an issue twice a month and charged 25 cents an issue. I had about twenty-five subscribers as I recall. Back in the '60s, that amounted to satisfactory disposable income, but my second business really got me excited about making money.

I was nine or ten years old when I had the brilliant idea to stencil home addresses on the curbs in front of the neighbors' houses so the addresses could be seen more easily from the vehicles of guests and postal carriers.

I went door-to-door asking folks if they'd like to have their address stenciled on the curb, $3 to stencil the address on one side of the driveway and $5 to stencil it on both sides. On the first day of business, I made $90! I still remember that figure, which back in the mid-60s was like making almost $800 today—not bad money for a grown-up, let alone for a kid.

And so, the next day I went door-to-door down a different street, and I made another 80 or 90 bucks!

Wow! I thought. *I'm making great money!* It was difficult to not get excited about that.

Back to that selective reflection of mine…

Naturally, like any good money-driven business person, I thought, *you know, what could really be awesome is if I could spend less time doing the dirty work and more time racking up sales.* So, I hired some of my fellow fourth-graders to do the stenciling. I ran them through a quick orientation, and dedicated myself to the sales end of the business. And I thought, *you know what? This is going to be my new job! This is quite possibly what I'm going to do the rest of my life!*

But then we got a complaint—careless, sloppy work from one of my employees.

Apparently, my new-employee onboarding process left much to be desired. I got a little caught up in how much money we were making, and it cost us in terms of the quality. Once the complaint came in, my father stepped in right behind, and simply said, "Okay. That's it. No more of this."

Chapter 2

EARLY INFLUENCES: AN INTRODUCTION

I've had the good fortune to have many people in my life who have served as models, teachers, mentors, and coaches, and the first of them was that man who ended my career as a stenciling man.

My father was a Marine aviator, which came with a lot of positives I tried to absorb. A phenomenal leader in many ways, he was a helicopter flight commander who taught countless people how to fly. Most of the kids he trained were headed off to Vietnam back in the '60s and early '70s. He was a great dad. He was a dedicated parent, a great teacher, and a hard worker. He believed in work. He was always active in my life, and one of my earliest baseball coaches. He provided for us, he protected us. But I'm not the first son of a marine father to say one of the negatives that came along with it was always his "My Way or The Highway."

As it is with most of us, my father had a colossal influence on me. I looked up to him. I learned from him. I wanted to make him proud. I watched what he did, and I emulated him in many ways. And when you look up to your father, it's not always easy to see all the layers and complexities to him. It's not so easy to distinguish the positive from the negative, to pick and choose which of his qualities to take on and which to discard. And so, I took on many of his good qualities. I took on his belief in hard work. I took on his desire to do a job and to do it right. I took on his interest in learning and in teaching.

But I also took on his belief that it was "My Way or The Highway."

After my brief lucrative career stenciling curbs, there was no end to other work. I hauled hay, I picked peaches, I worked the graveyard shift at a *Mars Short Stop* through college, I worked in the oil and gas industry. I liked work, and I liked making money, and I always outworked my spending habits—so I was able to see the fruits of my labor grow.

No doubt about it, the greatest influence in my early days as a dentist in the United States Army was a full colonel named Paul Cryer.

Looking back, now, I know that I had an amazing situation in the military. Colonel Cryer understood people, and he set me up for success. As a senior officer, he saw something in me, and though I was only a young captain and just beginning my dental career, he took me under his wing and we soon became great friends.

One of the primary things he taught me was that one of the benefits of working hard was getting to play hard afterward. He taught me that working hard allowed you the opportunity to do things that others don't get to do.

He also brought a joyful spirit to the work itself. Colonel Cryer would motivate me with challenges. He would say, "Bruce, I'm going to beat you today. I'm going to see more patients than you," and I would say, "No way, Colonel," and he would say, "Nope, it's a fact," and I would say, "That ain't gonna happen today, Colonel."

Now, Colonel Cryer might have had that same relationship with any of his doctors; he challenged all of us, but I was at his side more often. The other officers had been there a while, they had higher ranks, and had to go to more meetings than I did. I had just come back from Korea and was hungry to learn as much as I could. I was doing a lot of dentistry and learning a ton and having a ball. Pretty early on he gave me expanded duties in the army, and I built a great team around me. We were instrumental players in the productivity of the clinic.

But one of the smartest things Colonel Cryer could have done for me as one of my earliest mentors started with a question he asked me one day.

"Where do you want to go next month?" he said.

"What do you mean?"

"Well, there's a dental course here in Texas," he said. "And there's one at the Presidio in San Francisco, and there's another one up at Walter Reed in D.C. So, you pick it. Wherever you want to go is great with me."

That was an early and brilliant gesture because, at the same time he was recognizing me for my work by presenting the opportunity to travel and learn as a reward, he was also attaching paramount significance to continuing education.

Leaders who are focused and visionary aren't always equipped with softer skills; we all know the stereotype of hard-edged and unbending military superiors, but one of Colonel Cryer's best qualities was his affability. He could light up a room, converse with anybody, and he wasn't afraid of developing and maintaining personal friendships with the people on his team. But watching Colonel Cryer go about his work with a spirit of joy and infectious affability whether he addressed a member of his team, one of his superiors, or one of his patients. There was no rank when it came to being human. Everyone deserved that smile.

I served under Colonel Cryer's leadership from 1980 to 1984, and through that process, I felt I accrued a great deal of valuable leadership skills—how to work with people, how to engage with others, and how to develop an appropriate bedside manner. I had the opportunity to work with some of the best dentists, prosthodontists and oral surgeons in the military. I got to pick their brains and learn from all of them. They were all early mentors to me.

You would think, with all that hands-on dentistry and continuing education, working with great dentists and mentors,—especially as a protégé of Colonel Cryer—that I might have left the army and gone into private practice fully prepared for the hallowed halls of legendary leadership.

I certainly felt like I was ready for it. I had the skills and the experience.

But something happened on the journey from that award-winning, 28-chair army clinic to my own private practice.

Suddenly, I had responsibilities I never had in the army. I was responsible for hiring, training, and developing a team. Now I had finances to worry about—the stress of debt, overhead, office management. Despite the confidence born of my early success as a fourth-grade entrepreneur, the stakes were now much higher. I was doing it in a new arena, it was my business; and what added to the ever-present concern of making enough money to provide for me and my family was the fact that now I had to worry about making enough money for my team to provide for their families. This was brand new territory.

I was working from a *scarcity mindset* (something I'll address in greater depth in a subsequent chapter of this book) and what got lost in the dust storm of all those stressors? The greatest lesson I thought I had already absorbed from Colonel Cryer—how to treat the people on my team.

All the old habits came back. Those less attractive tendencies I can turn back to if left unchecked. If I was upset with any number of things that might go wrong in the course of a day—a patient with a complaint that revealed a flaw in the practice, the front office assistants who irritated me with how they answered the phone, an assistant who deviated from a system I thought we had established—I wasn't inclined to have a conflict conversation with them, I didn't like conflict. I kept all of the little irritations bottled up inside and stuffed each new annoying incident into the bottle until it got so packed with toxic elements, it was bound to explode. I was a walking time bomb. That's just how I was. It was the way I handled things.

There was a right way to do everything and there were plenty of wrong ways. Everything was black and white. I settled into the "My Way or The Highway" position; it was the stance I knew best. I had witnessed it all through my formative years. In a way, it's easy, right? It allowed me to ignore the real problems—the breakdown in systems, my flawed training techniques, the missteps in communication. If everyone just did things my way, everything would be great. The money would flow into the coffers in buckets.

The worst part of that approach, though—and this is the thing I needed to realize before I could correct my direction—was my neglect of the personal lives of my team members.

Though I had a great mentor in Colonel Cryer, who could give clinics on interpersonal relationships and team building in his sleep, stacked against those crushing pressures of my early years as the owner of a clinic, the pressures won. I stood alone in a mess I had created, belting out Frank Sinatra's "My Way" so loud I couldn't hear the sky falling down. I sang that song more than a dozen years before I realized I needed another approach, that nothing I was doing was anywhere near legendary.

Long story short, I finally stopped singing that song, and my hope is that this book has come into your hands at a time in your career that doesn't seem as dismal as my early days in private practice, but I'm confident that, wherever you're at in your career—whether your track record as a leader is pockmarked and scarred or filled mostly with successes—you'll find something in these pages that brings you and your team some comfort, some hope, some new ways of looking at old problems, and at the very least, some understanding that you're not alone on this journey.

Chapter 3

THE PARABLE OF
SMILEY FACE/FROWNY FACE

It's not that I wasn't reflective in my bad-boss days. I thought all I did was reflect! I reflected on how much money I needed to make. I reflected on all the things that were holding me back from having the best dental clinic in Texas: the terrible phone demeanor of the front office assistant, the cleaning company that used a whisk broom to clean the carpet instead of a vacuum cleaner, the hygienist who was always in a hurry, the new dentist whose work was a little sloppy, the patient who was nasty to everyone on the team but was nice as pie when I walked in the room … I thought I was Doctor Reflection! It just happened to be that I was Doctor Selective Reflection.

Selective Reflection is a term employed by disciplines ranging from communication to psychology to physics, but for our purposes, I'd like you to take it at its textual level by comparing it to *selective hearing* which refers to limited hearing. Similarly, *selective reflection* is limited reflection—limiting your reflection to the external, to everything outside of yourself, to all those things around you that you *think* are holding you back from astounding success.

In those early days, the problems were always everyone else's fault, rarely my own. The only thing legendary back then was how everyone else always fell short. I didn't reflect on the things that were most likely positioned to fix the problems. I wasn't participating in *self-reflection*, which, as it turns out, is a fundamental requirement for good leadership.

I could point to any number of occasions and experiences—most of which are in the shape of mistakes, mishaps, and setbacks—that set me on the path to self-reflection, on the real reflection necessary for good leadership. But one story stands out to me for the myriad lessons it taught me about the value of self-reflection.

I present it to you here, early in our work together, to suggest its paramount importance for understanding everything that comes in the subsequent chapters.

I didn't want to admit this then, but for the first decade and a half in my practice, no one liked working for me. People hated being there. This is the experience that slapped me in the face with one of my major personality traits. I had an attitude when I walked in the door and it was often at odds with what I wanted out of my dental career.

I had loved my time in the army as a dentist in that 28-chair clinic under Colonel Cryer; it was fun and exciting, and every day was a learning experience. And when I started my own practice, I wanted that fun and excitement and continuous learning to be a part of every day. I wanted to have a model practice, and I wanted that practice to be something I could be proud of—something I could even one day share as a kind of teacher for other dentists.

And I wanted to teach. I loved teaching. Somebody told me years ago, if you want to teach, be the best that you can absolutely be—do something, and do it to the best of your ability—and then share that with other people.

Well, the first fifteen years, I wasn't doing a very good job. I guess because I truly tried to come in with an attitude that this was going to be a great day, it was difficult for me to see that I was coming in with an attitude, with a chip on my shoulder. And I wasn't aware of it until I started paying attention to a little game my team had been playing on me for some time.

Somewhere along the way my staff members started posting a drawing of a face in the break room. "Despite my thinking that I pad an eagle's eye attention to detail—especially when there was a patient in the treatment room—I guess my attention to detail was not always so great when it came to my employees. And so, it took a while—maybe three years or so—for me to finally notice this drawing of a smiley face that someone posted in the break room. And I thought, how nice! Someone put up a smiley face. What a lovely, thoughtful team I had working for me.

Who knows how much time passed before I even looked up again to see if the picture was still there, but one day I went into the break room and I noticed it again, but this time it wasn't a smiley face; it was a very cartoony-looking frowny face, and I thought, *Hmm, I wonder what that's all about?*

Well, of course the phone started ringing again, and a patient in room two needed to be sedated, and another one was complaining about a scheduling issue, and another one was a no-show, and the checks needed to be written, and all of the demands of the day replaced my curiosity about the cartoon faces in the break room, until I looked up again one day and the smiley face was back again.

And every now and then I would walk in and mean to ask someone about it, but maybe no one was in the break room at the time.

And so, one day I finally walked in and Sommer was there, and I finally asked about it.

"Sommer, what's the deal with that drawing there on the board? Sometimes it's a smiley face and sometimes it's a frowny face."

And Sommer said, "Well, you need to talk to Gaye about that."

And so, I went and asked Gaye, and she said, "Well, now, you need to ask Emily about that."

And so, I went and talked to Emily, and Emily finally said, "Well, Dr. Bruce, that face up there is you."

"What?"

"Yep. That's you," she said. "When you walk in the office every day, whoever sees you first measures what kind of mood you're in, and then we come to the break room and we either put the smiley face or the frowny face up on the board so that everybody knows which Dr. Bruce we're going to be dealing with that day."

And I chuckled and said, "You don't really do that, do you?"

And she said, "Yep. Every time you walk in the door."

Of course, I knew that I wasn't always a bundle of joy to be around. I mean, I was the boss, wasn't I? And as the boss I had to deal with issues no one else on the team had to deal with, didn't I? Didn't people understand that it wasn't all about roses and pink lemonade every day? Didn't they realize that every day I walked into the office with a smile on my face, ready to take on the world, and that on those occasions that I was cranky it was *their* fault? *They* were the ones who were responsible for the frowny face. In fact, I was convinced on some days that everyone on my team was there for the sole purpose of ruining my day.

Well, I couldn't shake that story for a while, and the reason I go back to the parable of the smiley face/frowny face as a kind of watershed moment in my development, not only as a leader but as a human being, is that it contains a number of lessons for me.

The first thing it brought home to me is that I had an effect on others. How I walked into the office every day, how I showed up and presented myself, had an impact on others, as well. Even though I thought of myself as having a pretty positive, cheery disposition, it was clear to me now that my team didn't know what kind of a boss they were going to be dealing with from day to day. They breathed a sigh of relief on my good days, and on my bad days they walked on eggshells and kept their fingers crossed that tomorrow would be a better day. And if I continued to walk into the office with the attitude that everyone showed up just to piss me off, I would never be able to see what was actually happening—that they were coming in to work trying to do a great job, and that maybe my attitude was making it difficult for them to do that. At the very least, I wasn't recognizing their value as members of the team.

Another thing this story taught me is that not everyone on my team was willing to tell me the truth about the smiley face/ frowny face. I went to three people before I finally found some-one who felt comfortable enough to tell me the truth. What did that say about the responses I received from Sommer and Gaye? Clearly, they felt less comfortable speaking to me than Emily did. Emily was the office manager and had been with me a long time by then. The others were a little more tentative.

Maybe there was something about me that precluded people from getting comfortable with me until years and years had gone by. Were they afraid of my reaction? Well, I didn't have to reflect too long on that before realizing that this was not the kind of boss I wanted to be.

I also realized that even though Emily was the only one willing to tell me the reason for the smiley face/frowny face, the fact that they posted it on the break room board for all to see, suggested at least some level of comfort and security with me. And maybe they actually *wanted* me to see the drawing and acknowledge it far sooner than I did. Maybe they were actually expressing a desire to let me in on a little secret about myself in a harmless way, in a way that actually might help my understanding.

In the days that followed, I poked fun at myself a few times by bringing up the smiley face/frowny face story and noticed, immediately, a new lightness in the office, a lightness that reminded me of those days under Colonel Cryer's tutelage. Even though I had always thought of myself as fun-loving and informal, I was learning how important it was that my staff felt comfortable and secure around me—that a casual and lighthearted disposition did not take away the seriousness or the professional demeanor expected of a leader.

And before long, it wasn't uncommon for Sommer to pause after I barked about something, and to look at me sideways and ask if I had taken my meds today?

It's always enough for me to stop in my tracks and say, "Sorry. Am I being a butthead again?"

And very respectfully, they'll say, "Well, I don't want to—you know, say that exactly—but you might want to do a little gut check here today."

And we're able to laugh it off a little, but just calling my attention to my attitude gives me an opportunity to stop and name it, and most of the time it's enough to help me realize I'm not on top of my game, or that something's bothering me and I'm taking that emotion with me into the office.

I began to reflect more closely on my moods after the smiley face/frowny face experience. I wondered if this not only occurred for me, but did it occur for the other team members? And I noticed it did. This may seem obvious to everybody else out there, but the experience made me realize how important it is to observe the people around me more closely.

I'm thinking about a very hard-working and conscientious employee of mine who used to come in every now and then, and boy, she just was not in a good place. I mean, she was snapping at everybody, and everybody was kind of walking around her very gingerly, and I would go to her on one of these days, and I'd say, "Hey, how you doing? Is everything okay?

And she'd say, "Yeah, why?"

And I would say, "Well, I don't know. It just seems like you're upset about something. Is there anything I can do to help?"

And invariably she would say, "No, no, I'm fine. I'm fine. Thank you for asking."

And that simple, genuine gesture, just asking if there is anything you could do to help a coworker can have a strikingly positive impact. Sometimes that's all it takes. It's not like you're going to magically fix everything, but often enough, even if they are deeply upset about something, simply asking if they're okay, or if there's something you can do for them becomes an opening, an opportunity for them to share with you and maybe ease a bit of the burden.

Often enough, we don't even know what it is that's bothering us. Maybe we just wake up in a funk and come to the office under the power of some general malaise or irritation, and all of a sudden, if somebody cares enough to ask, "Is everything okay?" it's enough to help you take stock of the morning and reflect a little bit more on where the irritation is coming from. Maybe it was a tough phone call, bad news from an old friend, a physical ailment, maybe you left the house a little sore at someone in your family, or you feel like you're falling short everywhere. Maybe you felt like you handled a situation poorly or you've got a difficult phone call to make later in the day. Simply reflecting a bit more deeply on the issue is often enough to help you figure things out.

My team retired the smiley face and the frowny face, after I promised to commit myself to smiling a bit more, but I still point to that experience as one that really helped me change the way I thought about how I showed up every day. It didn't mean that I put on a fake smile before I walked into the office, but it did help me to learn how to check in with myself if I did wake up on the wrong side of the bed. It was one of those experiences that led me to see the profound value and paramount importance in real reflection.

And, as I touched on above, legendary leadership doesn't happen without real reflection.

LESSONS ON
LEADERSHIP

This is neither the first nor the last time you'll hear me say that legendary leadership doesn't come without real reflection. And any number of events or experiences are capable of urging you toward genuine reflection. I suppose the most fortunate among us are gifted with the capacity to look at their lives and circumstances with objectivity. Maybe they're born with it, or are lucky enough to be reared in a family that nurtured and cultivated it. Perhaps an early experience is responsible for its presence in their lives.

For others, the capacity for reflection comes from learning from those who have come before us, from reading, studying, and scholarship.

For many of us, though—maybe even most of us—the catalyst for genuine reflection comes in the shape of mishaps, mistakes, failures, and accidents. And for the hard-headed among us, these mishaps, mistakes, failures, and accidents often have to pile up before we understand the real value of reflection.

But if the capacity for it comes by way of something we might call *failure*, then maybe we have to redefine *failure*, or put in quotes and italics, because it seems a misnomer to give a bad name to the thing that wakes us up.

In the end, I'm not sure it matters much how we come to learn the importance of genuine reflection. What is more important is that it comes.

What follows from this point are some of the more important lessons I've learned about legendary leadership that only come when the reflection shifts from selective to genuine.

Chapter 4

SCARCITY, ABUNDANCE

I would not have had the language for understanding the issues that were holding me back from legendary leadership in the early days of owning and running a dental clinic, but when I look back on those days now, I can't help but realize I was operating from a *scarcity mindset.*

By the time this term, and its opposite, the *abundance mindset,* were coined by Stephen Covey in *The 7 Habits of Highly Effective People*, I had already been a bad boss for about five years and would be unfamiliar with the idea of scarcity and abundance for a few more years. Over the past several years, though, it has become overwhelmingly obvious to me that understanding these concepts is paramount to a deeper understanding of leadership.

There's no end to the amount of material out there on this topic of the scarcity and abundance mindsets. The concept appears in articles by everyone from people in business and finance, to scientists, politicians, educators, anthropologists, psychologists, economists, and beyond.

A simple online search for information specific to any of these fields will yield seemingly endless results. But you don't have to move far beyond a simple definition of the words *scarcity* and *abundance* to begin to see the impact of this notion on leadership.

Scarcity refers to a kind of shortage—the state of something being scarce, or in short supply.

I've played and coached many teams in a variety of sports over the years, so, in order to briefly explain these mindsets, I'll turn to an analogy that comes pretty easily to me: the pizza party.

As a player and coach, and even as the host of countless sleepovers, I've been on both the giving and receiving ends of countless pizza parties.

Let's imagine you're a child at a pizza party celebrating the end of a season for your team or club or organization. The kids are all hungry, of course (because they're kids), and the delivery person from the best pizza joint in your town drops off the pizzas on the banquet table you set up in the community center.

Regardless of whatever shenanigans the children are participating in when the delivery person arrives, they will certainly notice the arrival of the pizza before any of the parents notice.

The children on the team—let's just say they're all operating from a scarcity mindset—they have already counted the number of pizza boxes, and they're a little angry that you, the coach, have only ordered three pizzas, and very likely, because you're a grown-up, you've probably made the mistake of ordering at least one vegetarian pizza. That means there's probably only one sausage pizza and one pepperoni. They've also counted the number of children present, and looked around to see who their greatest competitors are for the very finite amount of good pizza available. Of course, they rush to the table (no one is thinking about the two measly liters of soda you ordered yet) and grab a slice of pepperoni or sausage pizza, not thinking or caring about the damage the steaming hot pizza is going to do to the roofs of their mouths; not caring that they're not even remotely chewing or in any way enjoying the pizza. They're thinking only of the great urgency before them: devour this first, burning hot piece of pizza or you'll have no chance in hell of eating a second piece.

That's what it's like to eat pizza when you're operating from a scarcity mentality. There's only so much of it to go around, and everyone is a competitor for that finite amount of pizza. There's no room for generosity here. No room for a profound enjoyment of the best pizza in town; there's not even the possibility of an equal distribution of the pizza. And no one but his mother has even noticed two of the most disturbing casualties of the celebration: 1) little Owen who is still trying to squeeze his way shyly to the table for a piece of cheese melted to the cardboard; and 2) the pizza delivery person who is lying on an empty pizza box on the floor, his nose bleeding.

Let's turn back to the moment the delivery person is just taking the pizzas out of the delivery truck outside the community center. And let's say there are two kids on the team who are operating from an abundance mindset, which they take to mean that there's plenty of pizza here for everyone (provided the grown-ups have been told the pizza is for kids only). One of these abundance-minded kids is Jessica, who plays shortstop, and the other is her twin brother, Tim, the centerfielder. They've counted the pizzas (3), counted the children (12), and they know, of course, as we all do, that there are eight slices of pizza in each box, and they've done the relevant math. Each kid can have two pieces.

Forgive me for the extra drama here, but because Jessica and Tim are operating from an abundance mindset—and knowing that they are aware of the kids in the room who are scarcity-minded—they pull the kids on the team together before the delivery person enters the community center, and they fill them in on the pizza math they've done, and they choreograph the order in which the kids can eat their pizza, shortest (Owen) going first, and tallest (Jessica and Tim) going last.

My point is that the only thing that can make the pizza party outcome good for everyone, is if at least one of the people in the room is operating from an abundance mindset.

Also, in this scenario, the delivery person is uninjured.

Returning to our purposes in our journey to legendary leadership, I know that I was operating from a scarcity mindset in those early days I keep referring to as my bad boss days. There was no end to the bills, there wasn't enough money to go around, there wasn't enough time in the day, and I was the only one with all the answers.

We're all susceptible to the scarcity mindset from time to time. It refers to a mindset, the guiding principle of which is *lack*. Something is lacking, missing, or scarce. You get so obsessed with whatever the greatest need is, whatever the greatest lack is, that it's hard to focus on any of the other things that are equally necessary to consider. And, no matter how hard you try, you can't shake the obsession.

A scarcity mindset refers to a mindset that is primarily driven by the lack of something—the usual suspects in the blame game of scarce resources are *time* and *money*—there's a lack of financial resources, a lack of time—but in the personal and professional space it might also include things like creativity, intelligence, and interpersonal relationships.

Think of a writer who is the victim of a scarcity mindset. Let's say he's a late bloomer who grew up in a house without books and now finds himself writing his first complete story at forty years old.

To take an example from an arena from the world of dentistry, think of a writer who, coming from a scarcity mindset, might be absolutely despondent after discovering that F. Scott Fitzgerald was only twenty-nine years old when his most famous book, *The Great Gatsby*, was published. If such a writer sees him or herself as limited creatively or intellectually, he may never get beyond comparing himself against all of the other writers in the world who were obviously so much more abundantly brilliant, gifted, skilled, and talented.

You can imagine such a writer saying something like what the writer Gore Vidal is credited for once saying, "Whenever a friend succeeds, a little something in me dies." There is some debate as to whether Vidal said this jokingly or not, but this is not an uncommon manner of thinking for the writer described above. For the scarcity-minded, the entire enterprise is likely to be marked by jealousy, competition, and insecurity. When we feel that money and resources and talent are scarce, it's easy to think of the people around us as competitors rather than people who are in on this together.

How often have we heard the joke of the diligent coworker being told to slow down, "you're making us look bad." Like many of the jokes we tell, there's an element of pure truth swirled in with the joke.

On the other hand, a person who operates from abundance, is never upset when someone else has more than they do or succeeds in some way. They are more likely to see potential as unlimited. A writer who approaches the craft from an abundant mindset recognizes herself and the others around her as having a great capacity for creativity and success.

It's not difficult to fathom the ramifications of a leader who is driven by scarcity, obsessed with the ways in which their business is falling short. It's difficult for the bottom-line obsessed boss to keep from championing that mindset among his staff. He harps and harps on the members of his team to produce more, work faster, work harder, work smarter, and so on, and everyone on the team feels that pressure. And what happens when the new front desk assistant comes along and falls behind in her work? If she asks me to step away from my work to help her, I just might feel the boss breathing down my neck with his *bottom line this, bottom line that* lecture, and I might feel that providing support to the new front desk assistant could only come at my own expense. And it's easy to see how this mindset could lead to a toxic office culture.

When we operate from a scarcity mode, we're *condensing*—we're becoming smaller in our lives. If I'm consumed with how I'm going to pay the bills in the short term, what can I possibly be thinking about all the things that are necessary for success in the long term? How can I possibly consider continuing education for myself and my staff? What happens to the coaching, marketing, and training that are so necessary to success? More likely than not, you view them as expenses rather than investments in yourself and in your team.

The adoption of the scarcity mindset is often more about perception than reality. We see it all the time. We look at the next-door neighbor in her new car and the crew remodeling her kitchen, and the architect looking over the addition plans with her in the front yard—we look at the clinic or the business on the other side of town and feel like they're living the dream—and maybe they are, but often enough they're killing themselves to keep up with the pressures.

And I can't tell you how many times I've consulted with doctors who think of themselves as mired in hopeless situations, when all they really need is to take a more realistic look at what they've got going for themselves. But it's easier said than done when you can't see anything on the table other than a pile of bills.

One of the risks in this conversation of scarcity versus abundance, is believing that the issue of scarcity and abundance is mostly financial. I would say that for many people who operate from scarcity, money is often the great obsession. And it's important, of course—if you or your business is financially insecure—to be aware of this, and to be realistic in your focus to turn things around.

But obsession over scarcity can take the mind prisoner and lead to tunnel vision, and tunnel vision can preclude you from attending to the myriad of non-financial issues that are equally necessary for success. Tunnel vision removes the clarity necessary to see all of the things you have going for yourself, that you consider to be a part of abundant living. For me, those include my family, meaningful work, recreation, seeing my buddies, going on vacation, and being a part of my church. There are times I can't imagine feeling better. And when I have that thought process, I often find that I'm keeping the door open for more good things.

But regardless of the lack of money, it's important to understand the value of an abundance mindset, to take careful stock of those things, tangible and otherwise, that you have in abundance.

And still, we can dip back into the scarcity mindset.

We've all heard the stories about the millions of Americans whose finances suffered when COVID-19 reared its ugly head. It's not hard to imagine how many mindsets shifted, if only temporarily, from abundance to scarcity.

I've mentioned earlier that I've always been confident that my ability to make a buck would never fail me. When my father lost his job about a month before I graduated from high school it would have been easy for me to fall into a scarcity mentality and fret over where the money was going to come from, but I felt if I needed more of it, I knew I could get it by working.

But as I also said above, being a business owner brought on a new set of concerns, rattling that confidence temporarily. I knew I could find a way to make money for myself, but going out and picking peaches again wasn't the financial solution to making my clinic successful.

And like many people, I've struggled with depression, and that can lead to a scarcity mindset as well. From time to time, I've had to put some effort into keeping an abundant mindset. A good therapist helped me to think of life as a giant quilt. You have all these patches that represent periods of your life; not every day will be filled with wonderful things, right? We go through life and we struggle through the valleys, we have to figure out how to deal with challenges. We have tough patches. And then there's great patches. And it's critical to our health and well-being that we don't put too much stock into the tough patches. We have to remind ourselves now and then that we're not defined by any single patch. Our lives are defined by all of those patches.

MAKING THE SHIFT FROM SCARCITY TO ABUNDANCE

For some people, the scarcity mindset is a temporary, fleeting experience. For real sufferers, though, it's something they need to put a great deal of effort into turning around.

So, what do we do when we find ourselves coming under the influence of a scarcity mindset? How do we shift from there to abundance?

Ask 100 scarcity versus abundance proponents this question, and you'll probably get a hundred answers. And if you ask me the question one week, you'd probably get a different answer than if someone asked me the week before. But what follows are some pretty valid behaviors that I've found beneficial, not only in helping me to focus on abundance, but in helping others make the shift as well.

REFLECTION

By now, it shouldn't surprise you that this shift can't happen without real reflection. None of the tips for shifting from scarcity to abundance will happen without it.

1. **Take an inventory** of those tangible and intangible things that you already have, that you worked for, fought for, earned, were blessed with—everything from your favorite shirt to that first

sip of coffee in the morning, to vacation sunsets, to the uncon-
ditional greeting from your dog, to your love for your friends
and family.

2. **Make a list** of the people you love, old friends, the college buddy
    you miss like hell and who you know would go nuts if he saw
    you tomorrow, that cousin who's crazy about you, and your
    spouse, kids and grandkids who have just discovered how great
    her food tastes. There are many ways to be rich.

3. **Take control** of the things over which you have control. Some-
    times it feels like things are out of your control. No one expected
    the world to shut down when COVID-19 clawed its way into
    our lives. Restaurants shut down, schools shut down, businesses
    failed. Dentistry was considered the most dangerous profession
    on earth. But it was an opportunity for millions of people to
    revisit their lives, to learn a new language, learn how to play an
    instrument, write a novel, reengage with family, take on a new
    hobby, renovate the house, or build furniture.

4. **Immerse yourself** in an activity that brings you joy, that you're
    good at, that reminds you of things other than the thing that is
    urging forth the scarcity mindset.

Think about your past successes. When you're in the throes of
a scarcity mindset, it's easy to lose sight of your gifts, your skills,
your talents, and your past accomplishments. Remind yourself of
them. Your baseball career might have ended after high school, but
life went on, didn't it? There are still goals to be reached, dreams to
be realized.

Put a new spin on what you've been thinking about as mistakes, regrets, losses, mishaps, misfortunes, and failures. Find the lesson in them. Find the message in them. Redefine them as opportunities to grow, to develop, to strengthen. Let them be steps toward the successes you know you're capable of.

5. **Revisit Failure**. Think about those things that may have appeared as failures, rejections, and disappointments in the past, but in retrospect actually opened new doors.

6. **Think of all the things you're grateful for**. Take some time every day to thank someone you work with. We have all worked with people who are stingy with praise, who seem to think that commending others for their work, effort, and assistance comes at a cost to them. It does not cost you anything to praise someone else. Praise and gratitude are not finite. There will always be enough to go around. You would be surprised how showing gratitude to another human being can make you feel you are coming from a place of abundance.

7. **Stop comparing** yourself to others. No one else has had your life. No one else can tell your story. You are who you are because of everything that has happened to you. Somewhere, there is an 11-year-old girl getting better grades than her college classmates. Somewhere, there is a seventeen-year-old switch pitcher throwing 90 mph fast balls. That's fine. They're awesome. There's room here for all of us. Stop comparing.

8. **Set** achievable goals for yourself.

9. **Read or listen** to podcasts.

10. **Seek out people** you know who seem to be living from abundance. Interview them. Tell them how you see them as abundant people. Ask them their secret.

11. **Recommit yourself** to excellence (More on this in Chapter thirteen).

12. **Invite** your clients, patients, students, etc., to provide testimonials for their experience with you.

13. **Recognize the valid worries** you have about where you and your team and your business are falling short. Sit down with your team and brainstorm realistic ways to get back on track.

14. **Do whatever you have to do** to shift your thinking from yourself to thinking about others.

15. **Take the opportunity** to participate in behavior that forces you to shift your focus away from the thing you feel is lacking and leading you toward a scarcity mindset. Take your assistant out for coffee and ask him to give you an update on his or her goals and aspirations. Ask him how his sister, his partner, his father, his son, his daughter is doing. Ask your hygienist if her son is still playing ball or acting or playing chess. It comes at no cost to you, because you're operating from abundance. Not only that, but you just also may be reminding them of the abundance in their own lives.

There's nothing like lifting others up to make you realize how abundant your own life is.

Chapter 5

MORE ON MENTORING

If you've ever had an MRI, you can understand how perfect a metaphor it is for the condition of tunnel vision. It's tough to think of anything else when you're in that claustrophobic little coffin. You can't see much of anything beyond the curved white ceiling of the machine six inches from your face. The unseen attendant in the room has reminded you twice of the importance of staying still. And though she has encouraged you to keep breathing, it feels at odds with keeping still. And, all of sudden, it seems that the only thing that will relax you is taking a deep, guttural, body-shifting breath.

That's what it can feel like to be consumed by whatever—a lack of money, personnel, time, resources—all of those limited things that immerse you in the scarcity mindset.

Think about a time when you were consumed with money woes, making ends meet, paying the rent, having enough to put a few gifts under the Christmas tree. Think about a time you worried about how that family vacation set you back. It's tough to think about anything else, right? It's tough to take the time to sit down with your front office assistant and ask her for an update on her son's health. It's tough to ignore the perception that your hygienist seems to be doing a lot more talking than cleaning. It's tough not to snap at your office manager for the scheduling snafu that set you back two times this week! *How many times have we gone over this?!*

Or think about any worry that consumed you for a while and then lifted for one reason or another. How good did it feel when the worry lifted? The next month came, business picked up and a couple of checks came in the mail. Things suddenly look brighter. It's a new world! And look at this! You notice the smiley face is back on the break room bulletin board!

Among the more profound byproducts of shifting from scarcity to abundance are the clarity and expansiveness that come with getting out of that tunnel. You can finally take a nice, deep, life-giving-breath. You see more clearly when the worry lifts. You're no longer held prisoner under its suffocating pressure. You start to see life more realistically.

When I finally pulled out of the tunnel vision of that scarcity mindset that held me back from being a good leader for my first dozen or so years as a clinic owner, I was finally able to reflect, genuinely, on the kind of boss I had become.

I had always thought of myself as cool under pressure. I was the guy you wanted if a moment called for urgency. If there was a disaster, I was your MacGyver. Somebody choking on a bone? Somebody in the middle of a heart attack or a seizure? Somebody in extreme duress? In need of CPR? I was the guy you wanted. I could make the difficult phone call, coordinate, organize, direct. I don't lose control; I don't lose my bearings. I become hyper-focused in those situations.

But God help you if you forget a mirror on the exam tray. That's where I would lose it. I would go nuts. It was the little things that could set me off.

Is that who I was, too? Was I that person who blows up at people? What about the other Bruce Baird (now that I think of it, it hints at Bruce Banner, the soft-spoken scientist harboring the uncontrollable green monster powered by rage, right)? This was clearly at odds with how I saw myself in most situations. If you see me on the golf course, or with my grandchildren, I'm a caring, loving, fun-loving person. Or if you run into me at the mall, or at the grocery store, I'm an outgoing, gregarious person. I love visiting with patients. I love working on my friends, and I love having a team that are friends.

The new capacity I had for more realistic reflection allowed me to take a close look at the me I presented at the office. Why was it that I seemed to slip into the character of that old Marine mentor father of mine, for whom there was only one way of doing things? His way.

Well, I can't blame it on him, right? I can't blame it all on a scarcity mindset. Love is a choice. Goodness is a choice. Decency is a choice. And understanding this allowed me the space to rethink the idea of mentorship, and now seems as good a time as any to spend a few pages addressing a few more elements of mentoring.

1. **No single person should carry the responsibility of being your mentor**. In retrospect, it seems obvious, right? You don't have to believe 100 percent in everything your mentors do as leaders.

I eventually came to realize that I didn't need my heroes to be perfect. Only with the reflection that came with a more abundant mindset was I able to see that I needed to be more careful about what I accepted from my mentors. My father is my best example. He was a great mentor and father in many ways, but he was complex and had his share of faults. He was stubborn as hell. There was a right way and a wrong way to do everything, and if you wanted to do something the right way, all you had to do was watch him and take heed.

And in the early days of running a clinic, when the going got tough, I found myself slipping into my father's stubborn, "My Way or The Highway" shoes, because he was simply the model with whom I had logged the most observation hours.

Everyone who has played sports has a bad coach story, and I have a couple of them from someone I would still call a mentor—my high school basketball coach. He knew the game of basketball thoroughly, and we loved him, among other reasons, because he wanted to win as much as we did. We worked great as a team under him. His motivational strategy, though—let's put it this way: he was not a motivational speaker. He was not an ambassador for positive coaching. He was much more inclined to put the negative swing on everything. It was a mentorship of yelling, fault-finding, and blame. Weirdly, it worked for me as a kid, but it probably wasn't that way for every kid. And it's certainly not the kind of leadership that creates positive office culture. But I probably picked up a few bad habits from him.

And Colonel Paul Cryer was absolutely solid through and through. I learned invaluable lessons as a clinician from the colonel and equally priceless knowledge about how to treat staff and patients. I'm the man I am today largely because of his influence. There wasn't anything about him that I wouldn't be proud of emulating. But he had a different situation. He ran a clinic in the military, and I could only learn so much about running a business from him. I had to look elsewhere to find guidance in that regard.

One way to be mindful of discriminating mentorship is to be realistic in your observations and assessments of character. Some of us are better judges of character than others. If you're someone who can find faults in others the minute you meet them for the first time, are you still able to see them realistically—in all their complexity? Or will it be difficult to see any good in them? Do you get starry-eyed the minute you come into contact with a hero of yours? And are you still able to see the humanity beneath the glitter? Or are you more likely to see them as completely infallible?

The tendency for many of us on the search for mentors, especially those of us with engineering in our bones, is to look for the person who checks all of the boxes—someone who is business-minded, someone who is a great teacher, a coach, an expert clinician, a humanitarian, a sage, hard-working, etc.

Another way to be mindful of discriminating mentorship is to think about is as more compartmentalized than general. It might have made the going a little easier in my case, for example, if I thought of my father as a work-ethic mentor, and not so much as a leadership mentor.

The graphic below might help illustrate my point. The terms below represent eight areas of life that are important to me. I've met a lot of fine people in my life who might serve as mentors to me in one or more of these areas, but I couldn't name a single person who could serve as a mentor to me in all of them. That's a lot to put on a mentor. But I could certainly rattle off a few names of people who have served as important mentors for me in each of the categories.

BUSINESS | FAITH | FAMILY

WORK/LIFE BALANCE | LIFE-LONG LEARNING | DENTAL CLINICIAN

FITNESS | WORK ETHIC

Looking at that category of faith, for example, brings to mind, Reverend Bob Holloway, another mentor. He was my pastor in the early-to-mid-80s. He's the one that got me to start expanding my reading outside of dentistry and business and leadership—books about compassion and love, books to help me through difficulties

I struggled with. I was looking for joy, but I wasn't good at experiencing it. And he helped me a great deal through counseling. He opened my eyes to different ways of thinking. And I look at him as a major mentor in my life. I would not be where I am today, without the people I'm talking about. And, you know, when everything seems like it's going south, when it's not going the right direction, when you can have somebody that you trust, that can give you guidance, that's a mentor. That's a leader.

So, where do your life interests lie? Whatever your interests—basketball, writing, visual art, cryptocurrency, birdwatching, photography, history—you probably won't have to go too far to find someone interested in mentoring you in any of your areas of interest.

2. Put yourself in situations rich for mentorship.

I'll spend more time addressing this directly, but continuing education opportunities are one of the more common arenas in which to find mentors. And I'm not just talking about the workshop presenters. I'm continually amazed at the attendees I meet at conferences. There is no end to the wealth of information in a room filled with professionals who are continually pushing themselves to learn and grow and develop in their field.

3. Always be on the lookout for mentors.

They can appear anywhere. Whenever I attend a continuing education conference or workshop, my eyes are open for people that I can find a way to orbit around. I'm looking out for expert clinicians, men and women with stellar business acumen, motivational and inspirational personalities.

4. Mentorship is a two-way street.

As I've mentioned already, it's important to be on the lookout for mentorship, and to surround yourself with people who can provide you guidance or direction in any area. But it's equally important to pay that mentorship forward. Think about the invaluable help you've received from people who have served you as mentors. Or, if you don't know the richness of having a great mentor, imagine how helpful it might have been to have had one, and be that mentor for someone else. As I mention above, there is no end to the need that people have for finding someone they can trust who can teach, influence, and guide.

5. Don't take your role of mentorship lightly.

Understand that if there's someone else in the room, someone else is watching you. I don't care if you've been a dentist for thirty years or for thirty days. If you're in a room and someone else is there— whether it's a more seasoned dentist, a hygienist, a dental assistant, a young patient, or the daughter of another dentist who's in the office for Take-Your-Daughter-to-Work-Day—if there's someone else in the room, there's someone who is watching you and thinking—not in these exact words, that "This person I'm watching is showing me one way to move through this world. This is a way to be." That's a lot of responsibility, and you can't take it lightly.

6. Mentors come in all shapes and sizes and ages.

They don't always look like Mr. Miyagi from *Karate Kid* or Albus Dumbledore from the *Harry Potter* series. And sometimes they come along when you least expect them. If your eyes are always open, a young dentist or a recently hired hygienist twenty years your junior might surprise you with a new way of thinking about something.

There are some people whom I look up to as mentors in personal relationships. I'm very fortunate in that my sons-in-law are also mentors to me. I look at how they treat my daughters. I look at how they respond to situations, handle problems, take care of their families, take care of people. These approaches to life are massively important.

And speaking of mentorship as having no age restriction, one of the things I love seeing now is so many young docs that have been through Productive Dentist Academy over the years. These guys are unbelievable leaders. And they're only four, five years into their practices! And I look at them and go, "Wow! I wish I would have had those kinds of leadership skills when I first started out."

Fortunately, it's never too late to become a great leader. Yes, it comes easily to some people; but some of us are harder headed than others. And once you learn some of the tricks, it gets easier.

7. Refrain from comparing yourself with your mentors.

I know what you're thinking. This was the piece of advice I gave you in the section on abundance versus scarcity. Well, it's equally important here. I'm thinking about Carl Misch, who served as another significant mentor. Carl was actually my dental assistant during the first sinus graft I ever did in 1987. I can still remember my hand shaking and him telling me to hold the osteotome still as we were tapping on the sinus membrane, and I said, "I'm trying, Carl!" I was just shaking while we are fixing to tap a hole in this guy's head.

But Carl was so intelligent. He had a photographic memory, and everything he taught was backed by literature. I loved the structure of his teaching process. You could almost see how it was organized.

He was a mentor to me and was an infinite source of information. He had all the answers. And I recall wanting to be that for my team. Early on I wanted to do everything myself, I wanted to be the source of *all* the information because I thought I could control that.

But Carl Misch was a completely different person, with a different skill set, a different mind. I had to learn the importance of being a *source* of information for my team, but not the *only* source.

Teachers can feel this way sometimes. Classroom teachers can sometimes be rattled when a student asks them a question they're unable to answer. They may feel that their authority is in question if they don't have all the answers. But think about the value that can be gleaned from a moment when a student or employee asks a great question that you don't have an answer for.

Knowing where to find the answer can be just as effective as having the answer ready for them. It suggests the importance of continually learning, continually educating yourself. Telling that student or employee that you're a bit puzzled by the same thing can become an opportunity to learn together.

So, challenge yourself to be on both sides of the mentorship street. No matter how brilliant, wise, or old you are, always be on the lookout for legendary mentors. And always be aware that you can be that legendary mentor for someone else.

Chapter 6

ASSEMBLING AND DEVELOPING AN EXCELLENT TEAM

One of the most common topics we address at the Productive Dentist Academy, at all of its myriad levels, is the concept of *team*. There's no such thing as the *perfect* team. One problem inherent with the term Perfect Team is the great unlikelihood (and perhaps the impossibility) of more than one team holding the perfection designation.

But, the best reason for dismissing *perfect* as the goal for your team is that every team is comprised of humans, and as much as some of us maybe think we're close to perfect, let's face it, we're human. We're fallible. Put any two of us together in an office and give us a task, and our chances of conflict double. Throw in an intern, a headstrong veteran hygienist and another one straight out of school, a treatment coordinator, an office manager, a grumpy old-school dentist, and another fresh out of the University of Gothenberg, and a clinic owner raised by a Marine, and perfection seems like it's light years away from a long shot. Perfection is limited to the arena of dreams.

But *excellence* is something we can reach for.

We can't talk about *team* without addressing all of its inherent elements, from roles and responsibilities to conflict management to alignment of goals. In this chapter, we'll take a look at the various facets of team building, and what it could look like under legendary leadership.

HIRING FOR EXPERIENCE

I'm not sure it goes without saying that the needs of the business and the climate of the times are the major forces that drive the hiring environment. My story is not the story of every new clinic, but there are lessons in it no matter how your business compares.

When my partner and I opened our practice in Granbury, Texas, in 1984, we started with four employees: a front office person, a dental hygienist and two assistants. We hired them because they were experienced, and they were available.

That small inaugural team worked out pretty well for us, but hiring for experience is not all it's cracked up to be.

There are some misguided tendencies that practice owners have with regard to hiring; and I'm not just talking about *new* practice owners—it can happen to the old-timers as well. We like to find candidates with experience. Pull up any random *LinkedIn* posting for a job, and you're likely to find long lists of the employer's expectations regarding experience, prior success, and systems proficiencies. I'm not talking here, of course, about educational history and certifications necessary for the professionals in your field, but for the professional staff that often make up the lion's share of our businesses.

Like many business owners—especially those who start out with little or no business experience—it seemed prudent for us to look for candidates who had experience not only at the positions we were looking to fill, but also with the tools and systems that were a part of our early days as a clinic.

For example, *Dentrix* is our current dental practice management software, and I'd be lying if I said it wasn't a plus if a candidate was a master at running *Dentrix*.

As I said, that first small team of ours served us well for a while. But then our needs shifted.

There were two extraordinary perks to our location: Granbury, Texas, was located in one of the fastest growing counties in the United States, and to add to that blessing, eight easy miles down the road construction on a nuclear power plant was in its advanced stages.

Most offices are lucky if they see ten or fifteen new patients a month, but a nuclear power plant with 16,000 employees driving past our office every day translated into 300 new patients a month. Within a year, we were growing so rapidly that we were hiring one or two new employees each month.

It may not come as a surprise to you that there was an extensive learning curve for me in the hiring arena.

I learned a great deal about hiring and building a team in those years of growth, mostly as a result of baptism by fire.

In the hiring urgency that our location urged forth, it was hard to pass up an experienced candidate when they came along. Their resumes rose to the top of the pile, and their familiarity with some element of the business was often all I needed to be convinced to hire them. I was capable of turning a blind eye to everything else but their experience.

That soon taught me a common drawback of hiring experienced candidates. Often, one of the marks of their experience is that they understand the environment they're walking into. They feel they know what the office is lacking, and they know—often because you let them know—what they bring to the offering. A natural result of that combination of knowledge can sometimes translate into the mindset that they were brought in to be the Balm of Gilead that would fix everything.

But we had learned a thing or two in those first couple of years as a practice. As time goes by, you grow more accustomed to the day-to-day operations, you gain a greater understanding of what needs to happen to raise your productivity and grow your business. You fine-tune your systems, and you come up with more efficient, more effective ways of doing things—whether it's dentistry or education or real estate or whatever field you're in. You put your own systems in play, and the team you've built to that point gets used to them and understands the role they play in the business.

I was less inclined in those days to run any hiring decisions past the members of my team, and what happened with some regularity is that I pulled in a new team member who thought he or she was there to show my team how to do things the right way, and we often found ourselves butting heads against those experienced hires who were maybe prideful of their experience, stuck in their ways, and reluctant to come around to new ways of doing things.

It soon became clear that one of the pitfalls of hiring for experience was the risk I ran of missing out on the exceptional hire who might have contributed measurably to an excellent team.

EXPANDING YOUR HIRING PRACTICES BEYOND EXPERIENCE

But we couldn't always hire for experience. When we opened, it wasn't difficult to find the small handful of experienced candidates we were looking for. But when our needs shifted from two doctors to seven, from four employees to twenty, we knew it wouldn't be easy to find two dozen new hires with stellar resumes and experience in our systems. If we wanted to grow, we couldn't be as finicky. Our hiring process had to change.

That happy accident in sudden and massive growth wasn't all peaches and cream.

We were forced to essentially quadruple our employee roster in short order, which meant we had to start looking at other factors outside of experience when we were looking to fill a position. What that soon translated to in that time of growth was this: if you were looking for employment in Granbury in the mid-1980s and you had a pulse, there was a pretty good chance you were going to be working for Granbury Dental Center.

That hiring frenzy helped me build a pretty solid list of what I would have called (back then at least, hiring *failures*).

Now, of course, I would see them as learning opportunities, but I had a limited selection of tools in my leadership toolbox, then: I pretty much only had a sledgehammer and one of those tiny little screwdrivers that jewelers use, and as I was still inclined to the "My Way or The Highway" approach, I mostly used the sledgehammer.

Some of them worked out so poorly, I started to feel I was just a rotten judge of character; I was a real picker. Some of those bad picks came in the shape of personality disagreements, poor bedside manners, office bullying, gossipers, troublemakers, uninspired personnel, time management issues, stubbornness, communication challenges, low employee engagement and motivation, rigid hierarchies, and poor conflict resolution.

We saw it all in those early days.

HIRING FOR PERSONALITY

Before you start thinking I was always going to be a hiring dumpster fire forever, I should say that one thing I've always had going for me was an unending and resolute search for a better way of doing things. That quality inevitably leads to late nights pondering and banging my head against a wall, but it usually leads to better ideas.

And I have to say that not everyone I hired turned out to be a mistake. I happened upon some employees that consistently put forth uncommon effort in their daily approach to their work. Some of these uncommon employees still work for Granbury Dental Center today!

For a long time, I was so hell-bent on hiring people based on their previous skill set, and what happened quite often is these experienced new hires had the tendency to do things the same way they had always done them in the past, which was usually not the most effective, efficient, or productive way of doing them, and it often bumped up against the systems already in place in our office.

And what occurred to me—thankfully before it was too late—is that the thing that so often separated amazing team members from the rest of the pack was simply personality. My best employees loved working with others, they looked forward to coming to work with their colleagues, they looked forward to working with patients, they could carry on lively conversations with complete strangers. They simply cared for others, wanted the best for their patients, their clients, their colleagues, and themselves, and they wanted meaningful work.

After many years in the business, I finally set my engineering mind to the side when it came to hiring. I stopped looking for the years of experience. I stopped looking for the employees that checked all the boxes, and I began to look for personality. Did they seem confident? Did they look me in the eyes? Did they smile? Were they capable of carrying on a good conversation? Did it already seem like they wanted to be there? Were they willing to help others?

It's great to have an office manager with experience, but I don't attach more significance to that experience than it deserves. It doesn't trump a charming personality, a gift for interpersonal relationships, and a love for people. If your hires are warm and outgoing and have strong organizational skills—if they're dedicated to taking care of people, the experience isn't necessary.

That's when the leader comes in with the commitment and training necessary to develop the inexperienced hire according to their expectations. If you've got all those pieces, you're on your way to bringing up your best office managers from within the ranks.

I don't mind having somebody come in who has little to no experience working with our software and other important systems. I don't mind if they have experience in offices wildly different than ours. And that could be anybody. It could be somebody from a grocery store, a bank teller, or someone who was working a booth at a conference.

One of the things that changed as I grew to more deeply understand the importance of team is the advantage in hiring people with great personalities, interpersonal skills, and organizational skills. I don't care so much whether or not they have three to five years of experience at a dental office. They could have just left a job as a teller at the bank or a waitress at a local restaurant. Case in point, of the three members of my team that have been with me the longest, one came from Walmart, one used to work in a veterinarian's office, and the third was a massage therapist. And I'm certain our clinic would not have been the success it was without them.

INVOLVE YOUR TEAM IN THE HIRING PROCESS

Lest you think I figured out a little something about hiring all by myself, I have to tell you that the only reason I came to any deep understanding of successful hiring practices is because I let go of thinking that I was the sole person responsible for one hundred percent of the hiring decisions in my clinic.

After taking 100 percent of the credit for the good hires, and 100 percent of the heat for the eventual fires over the years, it finally occurred to me that I needed to pull my team into the hiring process.

They must have been shocked when I came to my senses and invited them to weigh in on the hiring process for a new employee. I asked them to take the potential hire out to lunch, with the intention of getting to know them—to see if the candidate was someone they thought they could work with. It soon became the standard for all of our new hires.

Of course, if we get twenty applications for an open position, we can't take them all out for lunch; this typically happens a little deeper in the interview process. By the time this "working lunch" occurs, we've previously interviewed the candidate, provided them with a tour of the place, and maybe even had them shadow someone in the office who works in a similar capacity.

If the position is an opening for a treatment coordinator (TC), I invite our current TC, the office manager, and a front desk assistant, to take the candidate on a working interview. They take the candidate to lunch, they get to know them, and they come back and let me know how they feel about the candidate. They're not responsible for any formal response—just "Not going to work, Doc. This is absolutely not going to work." Or they come back and say, "Oh, we love this person. I think they'd be great."

There are often some unexpected benefits from this simple shift in the hiring process. Something happens when you involve your trusted team members in this way. First of all, genuinely asking them for their input in the hiring process, recognizes and acknowledges the value of their voice in the business.

For the cost of a simple lunch at the diner down the street, you've shared the responsibility of team building with the most trusted members of your team.

It extends the responsibility of the hiring beyond you. Now, it's not just you who is making the decision. It's not just you looking closely at candidates to assess how they might fit in with the office. You've got a number of other team members to help you in the process.

It's also an opportunity to express the importance of the hiring process to your employees. In effect, you're telling your team members, "You're already here. You're an important part of this team, and you deserve a voice in the expansion of the team."

That simple invitation also gives your employees a greater stake in the business. It raises their investment and forces them into a bit of self-reflection—an opportunity for them to look within and ask questions. For instance, let's say there's something about the new hire that just doesn't sit well with your treatment coordinator. Your TC is less likely to just dismiss the candidate if the other two team members at the lunch feel different about him or her. It urges your TC to look within, to find the language to articulate what it is about the candidate that doesn't sit well with her. Maybe it has something more to do with the TC than it does the candidate.

Nothing bad can come of the self-assessment born of an exercise like that.

The working lunch also gives the candidate the opportunity to get a closer look at what it might be like to be a part of your team. If you've got four team members who work together closely on a daily basis, it gives the potential hire a good look at what it might be like to work in the office. The interview is a two-way street—you're interviewing the candidate, and the candidate should be interviewing you as well.

We can all remember what it's like walking into the space of a potential employer. Sometimes it just feels right, and you can't really put your finger on why that is. And sometimes the opposite is true. So much of that has to do with the feel the candidate gets from the team that's already assembled.

If the candidate feels like it's a good fit and the team agrees, that's great. But if the candidate doesn't feel it's a good fit, you've still gotten your money's worth out of the team lunch. And often enough, however it pans out for the candidate, the team walks away from the experience a stronger team.

Chapter 7

PEOPLE AS ASSETS: TO KEEP YOUR TEAM, KNOW YOUR TEAM

One of the things I learned in my early days as a practice owner, when I was operating from a scarcity mindset, was that I was more inclined to think of *things* as assets than to think of *people* as assets. When you're driven by the bottom line, it's a natural tendency to look at things as assets. I've got my car, land, or home paid off—those are things we check off in the asset column.

But when we think of *things* as assets, it often translates to thinking of the people who work for us and the clients we serve as the *resources* we need to get the things we want.

In my early years as a business owner, that was one of my faults. I'm ashamed to say that I didn't even know some of my employees' names until they were with me for two or three years.

And if I don't remember their names, I certainly won't remember their kids' names, and I won't remember their stories—their struggles, their challenges, their hopes, and their dreams. Our connections will always be limited to the fact that I'm their boss and they work for me. And you know what? Then I'm pretending. I'm just going through the motions.

So, at some point, I stepped back and I made a change. I spent more time talking to my employees, asking them about their histories, where they grew up, how many brothers and sisters they had. I asked about their kids. I learned their kids' names.

I asked them questions. How's your son Bobby doing? I remember you telling me about his struggles in algebra. And how's Mary getting along with her new baby sister?

And while they talked, I just listened, and when we were finished talking, I jotted down notes to help remember them. It may seem trite—taking notes after having heart-to-heart conversations with my team, but this was new interpersonal behavior for me, and the note-taking helped to keep my focus on my team.

I tell doctors to do that same thing with their new patients—to find out about them, find things they have in common. Smile and listen, I tell them. Get to know them.

And what I needed to realize before succeeding, is that these folks have lives, they have families, they have kids, and how *they* do is going to affect how *you* do. It's going to affect everything.

And it's not something you can fake. That would never work. The change for me took place when I realized for the umpteenth time that I was literally struggling to remember the name of an employee that had been with me for more than two years. We had been spending as much time with each other as we had been spending with our own families. But I had immersed myself in the business and the bottom line so completely that I had lost sight of the reason I got into business in the first place: to help people and to make my life mean something.

I soon found that the more time I spent getting to know them, the more it seemed to add to the life and the success of the clinic.

Caring about your employees individually and as a team, caring about their families and getting to know them is critical to the team's success. The better you know your team and their family and the more you show concern and care for them, the more likely they are to stay with you.

And not only that, but what you're likely to experience when you treat your team as family, when you genuinely think of them as critical to the success of your business, you may start to witness what NFL coach Tony Dungy says in his book *Uncommon*. He calls it *uncommon effort*.

I'm always amazed at what people are willing to do for the team. About fifteen years ago or so, the computers went down at our clinic, and without telling me, my entire team came in and redid all of the books over the entire weekend. I showed up on Monday and didn't even know they had done this. Their uncommon effort was a show of love for our patients and for everyone on our team. They got it done. They did it on their own. I paid them for that uncommon effort, of course, but there was never a question from any of them if they were going to get paid for their work.

Another time, I went up to the office on a Saturday, and there was an employee in the equipment room cleaning and mopping on a weekend. I remember looking at the date on my watch, and I must have looked perplexed.

Mop in her hand, she looked at me and said, "I noticed this area was in need of some love," she said, "and I thought I'd come in and take care of it."

That's uncommon effort. When they know they're valued, when they're allowed to prosper, they adopt an organizational interest that you just can't teach, and they're willing to do just about anything for the organization.

So, ask yourself where you're at with regard to your people. Where might you be devaluing people in your treatment of them?

Consider your own family, your team members, your employees, your patients. These are the people who are providing the value, and yet sometimes we think more of them as resources to help us get the desired thing.

When *people* are the assets, and the resources and the tools become the *things* that serve the *people*—only then are you truly ready to invest in your team and in yourself.

By this point in my life, I no longer have to remind myself that it's the people who are assets; it's long been a part of my reality; but whenever I find myself starting to slip off the track—whenever the concerns of the business try to elbow their way to a higher position than the people—I still return to the mantra that helps me focus on the real bottom line: the people I love, the people I work with, and the clients we serve.

"Remember their names," I tell myself. "Remember their names."

Chapter 8

TRAINING: THE ONE CERTAINTY

I have often said that nearly everyone in Granbury worked for me at one time or another, and a good number of them—at least from the early days—are glad to have that experience behind them. If I knew then what I know now, I would have had other ways of working with some of the more challenging hires; but back then, I was more likely to send them packing rather than to work with them when any conflicts came to light. And I'll bet that probably 90 precent of the hires who didn't work out could have been part of an excellent team if I'd worked with them. But I just never prepared them to become great team players. I never gave them the chance.

What I've learned since then is that whatever the hiring needs and challenges of your business, whether you hire a hygienist with experience or someone fresh out of school, one thing is certain: you can't build an excellent team without excellent training.

Give me a candidate with a great smile, organization and inter-personal skills, and along with the rest of my team we'll give them all the experience and training they need.

I often tell a story about one of my hygienists who wasn't very happy about a new hygienist that we had hired. The hygienist's complaint was that the candidate "just doesn't do things our way."

But I really felt the candidate had the potential to be part of an excellent team. She had the right skill set for the job, she came highly recommended, and she was excited about the possibility of joining our team. She smiled, she conversed well with the patients she met, and everyone seemed to like her. It's just that her systems weren't aligned with the systems we had in place, and this piece was at the essence of my hygienist's complaint.

So, I pulled my hygienist aside and I said, "Well, now I know where you're coming from. Our systems are very important, and I appreciate your looking out for them."

And then I put her to the task. I asked her if she could do me a favor.

And my hygienist said, "Well, of course."

I said, "You're an excellent hygienist, and I like the way you work within our systems; you do things a certain way, and the candidate could learn from that. Can you help train her to be like you? Could you do that for me?"

Now, asking an employee or a colleague to do something for you touches on the relationship between the two parties; it suggests an invitation and a response, which, if accepted, suggests an agreed-upon course of action. Not to get too formal or serious about it, but it's a kind of contract between the two parties.

And maybe I caught her off guard with that question, but in any case, she said, "Yeah, I guess I could do that."

This invitation, in particular, served a number of purposes: 1) it was an affirmation of my veteran hygienist's value to me and the team; 2) it recognized the importance of the value she put on our systems; 3) it effectively positioned her in the critical role of mentorship;

and 4) it turned the issue from a potential conflict to an opportunity for growth.

And guess what? This new hygienist began producing very close to what our training hygienist was doing within a matter of six weeks.

Now, I could have just told our team, "Let's not forget who the boss is." I could have simply said I thought the new hire was really good and that I wanted them to welcome her as the newest member of the team. But instead, I used that opportunity to call attention to the value of my veteran hygienist, and during and after the six weeks of that training process, I took plenty of opportunities to tell my veteran hygienist that she was doing an excellent job training the new hire.

And isn't it more rewarding and more fun to help new hires become better?

MOVING FROM TIME = MONEY TO THE TRICKY CALCULUS OF TRAINING

There was a time in my career, as you can imagine, that I had no patience for training. If my assistant had trouble temporizing crowns, I was more inclined to roll my eyes and grunt and temporize the crown myself than I was to train the assistant properly. I often say God has a sense of humor because he gave me four daughters. I had to learn to speak a different language. A language, one of caring and love. This language or different way of vocalizing and reacting had to carry over to my team members as well.

For a long time, I was driven by the notion that Time = Money, and when that's the equation that underpins your leadership, it seems easier and more prudent to do the work yourself.

Now, I've always been pretty good at math, but because of the prominence I gave to that Time = Money equation, it was nearly impossible for me, for a good long time, to understand the tricky calculus at the core of training—namely, that it costs time in the short term, but pays off exponentially in the long term.

And it's astounding what happens when you absorb the life-changing belief that the purpose of life—work, play, and everything in between—*is people*, not things. And one of the remarkable effects that belief in people had on me was that I began to more deeply understand that tricky math about training.

I can still remember the moment when I actually made the *decision* to change my perspective on training. My assistant temporized a crown that wasn't up to snuff, and I fought the devil on my shoulder who wanted me to roll my eyes and sigh and point off on my fingers all the things that were wrong with it—right in front of the poor, horrified patient.

Instead of listening to the little devil on my shoulder, I took my assistant into the lab and said, "Hey, let's take a look at this." And I said, "You know, do you see how that edge around the margin is coming sharp and jagged and a little bit rough? I really want to make sure that those are really smooth because, you know, those edges can just really drive your tongue crazy."

So, I built that training into my schedule. I spent thirty minutes with her, and then after about six months, maybe it was twenty minutes, and then fifteen minutes. And before long I would actually take a look at her work and found it was beautiful.

"Look at the contacts," I said. "See how beautifully they're shaped? See the contours?"

I trained her on the anatomy of teeth. It was worth it to me, because then I could go in, prep the teeth, and walk out of the room, and she would take over, scanning, designing, milling. And I would check them—I inspect what I expect. (More on this idea coming up.)

And here's another remarkable thing that occurs when training became a standard for me: if the assistant ever had a question, she felt very comfortable coming to me and asking me questions. This was not the case when my go-to response was eye-rolling and guttural sighing.

It's imperative that my team is perfectly at ease coming to me and saying, "You know, Doc, I don't feel comfortable with this. I'm having a difficult time with that." Their experience with me taking the time and having a patient, teacherly approach with them, allows them to feel comfortable coming to me.

Now, my first fifteen years in practice, I promise you, they didn't feel comfortable coming to me. They didn't even want to talk to me. And the response of an employee who isn't comfortable coming to you with questions might surprise you. If the training and patience aren't there, the employee might be inclined to take on a task they aren't comfortable with, rather than risk an outburst from her impatient employer.

"I can do everything by myself," she might say.

I'd much rather my assistant come to me with questions than to take on a task they're not ready for.

As soon as I began setting aside that time for proper training, I started noticing that my leadership skills, my job satisfaction, and my ability to communicate with my own team got better. The habit of excellence started to become physiologic. It became a business standard in the practice, and it grew, and it got deeper and deeper and deeper.

And it continued to get better, and over a period of time, the reality that the people on your team are your family takes root—it deepens and extends beyond the simple coaching and teaching we think of as *training*.

We all began to notice that we were doing a far better job of taking care of patients. The thing that really hit me was taking great care of people takes care of money issues. Every year, we were able to look back and say that we were taking better care of our patients than we did the year before. And I was able to say I was taking better care of my employees than I did the year before.

It spreads beyond the chair, beyond the operatory, beyond the clinic, the office, and the business. Whether you're leading a team, coaching AAU ball, or helping your child with her homework.

Interestingly, at first, I had to remind myself of the delayed gratification of training—that it cost time now, but saved time later. But not long after I made training a critical element of my practice, I began to realize that the time spent training and educating my team wasn't a cost at all! The training itself was a reward! In fact, it dusted off the joy of teaching that I felt had always been at the core of my own interest in learning.

And I began to look for new opportunities to train, to teach, to develop and improve. I would set aside time to sit down in my office and look at all the people on my team and do my own evaluation—not an evaluation of them, but of my responsibility in their development. It became a calendared time set aside to ask the questions that became a standard of training.

"How can I help this person do better at what they're doing?"

"What can I do to get this team of three to train our fourth chairside treatment coordinator?"

"How can I invite everyone to invest more deeply in their work?"

"What can I do to make their work here more meaningful?"

But in order for training to succeed, you have to commit to it. You have to be committed to training your people. It won't happen overnight.

But once you show your faith in them, once you have them secure in their confidence and their skill set, you'll find that you've passed that commitment on to them. They begin to see the benefits of that commitment you've made to them, and they begin to see how the business is a growing business. They see their role in that growth. And they have the upside opportunity to continue to grow themselves.

Before your very eyes, you begin to see you are fostering an environment that grows the members of your team into long-term employees from this day forward.

EXCELLENCE: THE CENTERPIECE OF TRAINING

I'll address excellence in another chapter, but a brief mention of it can't be ignored here, because it must be the centerpiece of your training. You train your team so that the final results the patient (or client) gets is at the highest level possible. And it has to be done the way the leader wants it to be done.

TRICKLE-DOWN TRAINING

Now, that may sound like a remnant of the "My Way or The Highway" approach, but the distinction is that the leader is responsible for explaining the *why* behind their approach. It's training based on the *why*. I've always wanted to do things more efficiently, provide a higher level of care. I've always wanted what *we* do to be the *ideal* way of doing things.

I'm working on the assumption that the legendary leader is guided by a standard of integrity and excellence, a standard born of experience. If excellence is not the leader's goal, then legendary leadership will forever be unreachable.

Bear with me while I dip into the world of athletics for an analogy.

I played a lot of sports growing up, and I coached a lot of teams as I entered fatherhood. When a team is coached with integrity, excellence, and sportsmanship (which, of course, has its place in the office), you know the difference when you come up against a team that isn't coached with integrity and excellence and sportsmanship. When you observe the other team playing dirty or dishonestly, you can count on this fact: the shenanigans are being passed down from the top.

The converse is also true. When you come up against a team that is coached with integrity and excellence and sportsmanship, you know you've got your work cut out for you. And you can be sure that it's the coach who sets the tone for the team.

And it's the same when it comes to the leadership of your own team.

If your goal as the leader is to train your team so that your patients or clients are receiving care at the highest level, *and* you're leading with integrity, that leadership trickles down through the team.

The only way for me to see that excellence and integrity trickle down and become a standard for my business is to train them exactly the way I want. If I'm training an assistant to polish a crown, I want them to polish it exactly as I would.

The other great distinction between this approach and the "My Way or The Highway" approach is that if my true goal is to provide the best, most efficient care, then I have to be open to new ideas that might lead to more efficient care. I must be open to listening to my team put their dukes up for another way of doing things. My team knows, from the value I place on continuing education, that I'm aware of the expertise and vision of others. If someone on my team feels they have come upon a more efficient, higher quality way of providing care, they *know* that I am interested in hearing more about it and seeing it in action.

If you've done the work of hiring wisely, you'll have new people come in who have been trained well, and you've got to be open to what they're doing. It's a results-driven arena. I want to put that new idea to the test. If they're right, that's how we become better at what we do. If it turns out that the new idea is flawed, they'll know that I gave it a hearing with an open mind, and they'll know that I'll give their next idea the same fair hearing.

A perfect example is Sommer, one of my treatment coordinators, who does big provisional cases. I looked at her work one day, and it was phenomenal. And I told her so, and then I asked her to do a training for all the chairside assistants. I told the team I wanted them all to see what Sommer was doing.

That recognition and the extended duties you offer your team, come as no cost to you, and when your team recognizes your belief in them and responds by believing in you, the benefits are immeasurable.

Chapter 9

TRUST, BUT VERIFY

If you asked me at any given point in time, what my personal production per hour was, I could pretty much tell you, "This month I'm doing $622 an hour," or whatever it was. I could answer that question to the dollar because our office used a tracker and I saw to it that my trackers were filled out every day.

At the same time, I had an associate who had someone on his team doing his trackers, and he never checked them.

I would ask him, "What's your production per hour this month?"

"Oh, I don't know," he'd say. "It's pretty good."

He didn't know what his production per hour was because his tracker hadn't been filled out in six weeks. He couldn't possibly know. And yes, his team was responsible for that, but the fact that he wasn't looking at it, he wasn't verifying that it was being done on a daily basis, translated into it not getting done on a daily basis. It hadn't become a habit for his team.

And I know how that goes. It happened under my leadership in those early days, too. I would put a new policy or procedure in place in my office, and I'd say, "This is the way we're going to do re-care," or whatever. And things are moving along nicely and this is how it's being done for a while, and the pages fall from the calendar, and you have a meeting eight months later, and somebody brings up the topic of re-care. And you say, "Why are we doing it this way now? Didn't we address this eight months ago?" And they say, "Well, no, we did that for a while. But now we do it this way."

And I would slip into my *but I'm the boss* shoes, and say, "Well, wait a minute, last time I checked I was still the boss, so why are we doing it this way now?"

And on the surface, maybe it was because someone laughed off the new approach to re-care, or we brought in someone else who had a different way of doing it.

But, below the surface, the real matter was ineffective leadership.

Whatever system it is you want to have as a standard in your practice—if it's solid enough to install as a system, it's your responsibility to present the system to your team and then expect it to be addressed accordingly. But it's not enough to expect it to be addressed and implemented accordingly; you also have to hold your team accountable for it.

It's so easy now with cell phones, because you can put little reminders on your calendar that say something like, *ask the office manager about x, y, and z.*

Now, these are things that I *expect* them to do, and I'm pretty certain they're on top of the task, but I'm just going to ask them about it, anyway, so they know that it's important to me and that its importance is ongoing. And if she knows it continues to be important to me, she'll do it.

If I do my job right, and continue to impress on my team the value of the system or task, at some point in time, it becomes physiologic—it becomes something that's just part of their DNA. I won't have to look at my trackers with Sommer, anymore. She does it because she knows it's important.

I *trust* that they'll do it, and I continue to *verify* that it's being done. As I hinted at in the previous chapter, I *inspect* what I *expect*.

It's important, though, that I verify it in such a way that doesn't suggest I don't trust them. A lack of trust never enters the equation. I trust my team. But I know that it's human nature to take a shortcut (or to take something that seems like a shortcut), or to do something in a manner that seems like an easier way.

I know the temptation of "Nobody's looking, why not do it that way?"

So, I might say, "Those trackers looking pretty good, Sommer?"

It serves as a simple reminder that this task or that system is important to me.

The more you trust and verify in the early days of a working relationship, and in the early days of a new system, the less you *have* to trust and verify in the long run.

BUILDING THE TRUST OF YOUR TEAM

One of the ways of assuring your trusted team members that you do trust them is by engaging them in a conversation of the systems, the policies and procedures you put into place, and having a discussion with them about the *why* of it.

In the old days, I might have responded to someone who took a shortcut with the tracking system by pulling out my inner Marine and reminding them that I was the boss, but it's critical for the effective leader to not only remind them of the value of the issue at hand, but to have a conversation with them about the efficiency and effectiveness of the issue.

For instance, re-care, or how you work with hygiene, how you check hygiene patients, and how the patients are greeted at the front desk. Dentistry is not that complicated. We have systems in place for greeting patients, for productivity, for collections, for hygiene, and for re-care. We have a system for how we do our exams. We have a number of systems, but it's not like we have 400 different systems.

But when we do something new, we share it with our trusted team, we discuss its pros and cons, we put the practice in place, and along the way we verify that it's working. We verify that it's being done.

As a leader, you need to keep your eye on those systems. Keeping your eye on those systems may mean that you need to shift directions along the way, and say, "Gosh, guys, you know, I really thought this would work well, but I'm beginning to understand that there are some wrinkles to iron out."

And when these decisions to put new procedures in place are measured and thoughtful and reflective, my team members get to thinking, "Doc really does care about us. He's evaluating the systems, and he's asking for our input, and together we become part of a solution that's going to make a major difference in our business."

I've learned from everybody across the board in dentistry, and I know enough to know that there's no value in the "My Way or The Highway" approach. There never were just two ways. I'm continually changing and finding new ways of doing things. And I'm all ears when it comes to learning new tricks and finding more effective and efficient ways to do things.

And when you have a team that is 100 percent behind what you're doing, and they're doing it, and you're not micro-managing, but *verifying*—asking them questions like, "How are you? How are things going? Are you making those confirmation calls? Are you on track? Are you running behind? Is this working out? Can you use some assistance?"—they'll understand that these questions don't translate to a lack of trust. They're meant to verify, yes, but the impact of these questions on the team is that they also serve the purpose of checking in not only on their work, but on *them*.

There may be only fifteen things that you want to ask about, but make sure you do it every month. When you do that, you're going to find that the team understands these fifteen things are a big deal. They begin to understand that this is something that makes the office run efficiently, and they get to do so much more than most dental practices around the country.

So, if they're not doing fine—if they're running behind—they feel comfortable owning that, because I'm not just concerned about them staying on top of their work; I'm checking in on them personally, as well. And because they understand that—because they know that the team is there to support them—their honest feedback may lead them to provide valuable information that urges us to shift directions, to fine-tune our systems.

These changes in attention and behavior can make a huge difference in productivity, but more importantly, they make a massive difference in the culture and mood of the office, and in ways that make employees feel good about going to work. It gives them purpose and responsibility in their work. They're making sure that when patients come through the door they're getting greeted in a certain way, for example, because I ask questions about those things. And they're doing things at a high level, because I'm holding them accountable, and I'm communicating with them on a personal and a professional level.

Leadership comes with consistency, and consistency is a result of this major component of legendary leadership: Trust, but Verify.

Chapter 10

INVITATION TO A HAPPY PLACE

We're only on the planet for a short time. It's a flash. And I've gone through periods of time in my career where, you know, you face obstacles and you face difficulties, but you persevere. And that's something that's about your state of mind, it's about how are you thinking. When I look at the people that I surround myself with—my friends, my coworkers, the business people I deal with—I'm always evaluating their state of mind. What are they thinking? Are they happy here? And it's not always the case. Even if you turn out to be the best boss in the world across every facet of the business, from hiring to training to treating your employees like family—you can't control everything.

I had a hygienist once whom I knew very well. She was a personal friend, a great hygienist, and a gifted photographer—but she just wasn't happy at the office. In fact, she hadn't been happy for several years, and it caused a lot of stress—on the team and throughout the entire organization. Some days she would walk in, and she would just be amazing, though. She'd be upbeat and positive, and cheerful as can be. But other days she would come in, and she would be depressed or angry and short-fused, and so people were always walking on eggshells around her. But she had some personal challenges that made things more difficult for her, and she was good at her work, and as I said, she was a friend; and all of those things combined to make it hard for me to let her go, and so for a long time we tried our best to work it out.

But when I finally realized that things would not turn around, I pulled her aside and talked to her.

"You know," I said. "I don't think you're happy here." I said, "We're only on the planet for a short time. And, you know, I really want you to find a place that you're happy."

And she said, "Are you firing me?"

And I said, "Well, I'm not firing you. I'm just inviting you to go to your happy place."

And boy, was she livid. She left the room and slammed the door, and I thought, "Well, that's the end of that. I just lost a good friend."

But not long after that, she moved to Colorado and found a little place where she set up an independent hygiene practice. There was another space open right next door to her practice, and she set up a little photography studio next to her hygiene practice.

About four years later, I did a double take when I saw her walking down the hall of the clinic toward me. A little bit of the old walking on eggshells feeling came back, and my heart starting beating like mad, because I thought she might have come back to settle a score with me for letting her go.

But I'll never forget what happened when she came in. She gave me a big hug and said, "I wouldn't be where I am today, if you had not invited me to my happy place."

Well, you know, she was crying, and I had tears in my eyes, too. And we hugged and I said, "Thank you."

And she said, "No, thank you."

And so, I think a lot of times, we want to hold on to team members and people in our business that aren't a good fit for any number of reasons.

But everyone needs to find a place where they're happy. Everyone deserves happiness. And it may not be in your pocket to give it to them, but one of the worst things you can do as a leader or head of an organization is keep people on board who, through their conduct and their interactions with patients, clients, and team members—present themselves every day, in ways that are antithetical to what you want in your business.

We often go through our careers thinking, "Oh, I can't lose this person," or "I can't lose that person; they're so productive," Or "They've been here forever," or "They'd just be devastated if I let them go."

So, we continue to hang on to them, and we ignore all the difficulties that come as a result because we don't want to have that crucial conversation—even though it's clear that their effectiveness, their efficiency, how they work, and how they present themselves every day may be doing more damage not only to your office and your business but also to their own health and well-being.

I've learned a lot over the years about the hiring process. And when you bring people in, that decision should be to bring in a person who is high energy, a good communicator, and somebody who smiles a lot—even if they're not necessarily experienced chairside or experienced at the front desk—a person who just exudes confidence.

The decision to hire somebody in your practice is a major decision, because the better your team, the better your practice, the better your patients are taken care of, and the better everyone does financially. The money part is at the end, of course, but I want to go to work and have a great day. I want to feel good about going to work. I want to say I love my team; I love the people I work with; I love the people I see. I just love going to the office because of the people there.

What I've seen through coaching and running a business over the last thirty-eight years, is that the hardest decisions can create the biggest increases in productivity and climate.

Most dentists just put an ad in the paper and hire somebody that comes in, they stay or they go.

And the 80/20 rule can be applied here as well. Eighty percent of the problems in a business come from 20 percent of the employees.

It's important to everyone—to the person you're letting go, as well as to the rest of the organization,—that you're not afraid to invite a hire that doesn't work out to go to their happy place if it comes to that.

You need to take a gut check on yourself, too. Are *you* in a happy place? If not, the message I opened this chapter is meant for you, as well. You're only on the planet for a short time. Take some of that time and find a place that you're going to be happy. Surround yourself with people who have integrity and people who are upbeat and positive.

We're not all going to be upbeat and positive every day, but if you're a leader of a business, and if your goal is to give your clients and customers and patients excellent products and services, then all of your team members have to be pulling the rope in the same direction.

When you surround yourself with colleagues and friends who have sunny dispositions, you'll find their positivity infectious throughout the entire office. It'll increase productivity. It'll be something that you'll never be sorry about.

Like many of life's greatest lessons, this one was not an easy one for me to learn. Years ago, I had an associate who left the clinic to go to his own happy place, and he took eight of my team members with him, and together they opened up a clinic down the street. This guy was a producer and he took a major chunk of our productive team with him. This happened in August, and by January our team minus a doctor and eight former employees was doing more across the board than we were doing before my associate left.

Why?

Because we had a team that pulled together—a team with a common sense of purpose. And we were all in a happier place.

Chapter 11

CONFRONTATION MANAGEMENT

CONFLICTS WITHIN THE TEAM

That conversation I had with my hygienist in chapter twelve, in which I invited her to a happy place, was one of countless conflicts that are bound to occur in any business. Poor work habits, resistance to change, poor communication, mistakes, relationship conflicts, difficult patients, difficult customers, difficult clients—as soon as you think you've seen them all, a new one comes along. And if you're a "My Way or The Highway" kind of leader, any conflict on the list can drive you mad.

What happens to productivity when you walk in the break room and you're not in a good mood? What happens to productivity when you're irritated or aggravated by a disagreeable interaction with a patient, or when there are interpersonal conflicts on the team? It can put stress and pressure on the entire team.

So, what do you do when team members are upset at each other, or when any one of the endless things that can go wrong does go wrong, or when one of countless conflicts erupt?

In the early days, I was inclined to ignore conflict until it got so bad I couldn't ignore it anymore, and then I'd explode. And it won't surprise you to hear me say that the ignore-it-until-you-can't-ignore-it-anymore approach never worked out in my favor. But stubbornly, I stuck with it until I learned how to manage conflict through communication.

It took a lot of mistakes, a lot of explosions, and a lot of reading and studying about interpersonal relationships before my mind was opened to the magic of communication. It's all about opening the lines of communication—precisely the behavior I was so inclined to dismiss in my bad boss days.

I've come a long way since then, but despite the overwhelming evidence, the magic of confrontation communication continues to amaze me. Not only has it helped me develop into an effective manager of conflict, but it has made me more astute and perceptive at recognizing areas of potential conflict before they occur.

I'll provide a sample interaction that has played out countless times over the years. Let's say I've got a treatment coordinator named Charlie who has been walking around grumpy, aggravated, and frustrated all morning.

I notice it as soon as I walk into the office that morning, but it doesn't feel like the right moment to step in. Maybe I'm not sure, at first, and I want to see how it unfolds. Or maybe there are other team members around and want to wait for a moment when Charlie is alone.

An hour or so goes by, and I see that Charlie is still stomping around the office, not being their usual cheery self on the phone, and maybe snapping at a colleague for not wiping down the counter after leaving a coffee cup ring on it.

I would have ignored this behavior for the first fifteen years of running a clinic. But I'm a different person now. Now, I would find a nice quiet moment—maybe while Charlie is sitting down to lunch, or sitting in the break room rubbing a headache from their temples. I'm going to pull them aside and say, "Charlie, what's frustrating you?"

And Charlie might say, "Well, you know, it seems like I'm doing everything here. I'm doing this, and I'm doing that, and I can't get anybody else to help."

I might encourage him to talk to Shannon or one of the other members of the team, and say something like, "Shannon, you're awesome. You're running around, and you're always helping out here and there. Would you mind helping me with these particular things when I need help, and I'll help you when you need this?"

In this case, when another team member is involved (and there's almost always another staff member involved) you're not only opening up the lines of communication with the frustrated team member, but you're inviting them to open the lines of communication in an equally positive way with other members of the team.

Another way to handle these situations before they occur is by coaching your staff to train new members of the team even as soon as you've hired them. So, now Charlie tells the new hire on day one, "Look, sometimes it gets a little crazy around here, and when it gets that way for me, I'm going to tap you on the shoulder and ask if you can help me out. And when it gets a little crazy for you, I'm going to expect you to tap me on the shoulder and ask for my help as well. That's what we all do around here."

It's a way to handle the negative things that happen in the office now. And it's a way to handle them together.

CONFLICTS WITH PATIENTS/CLIENTS/CUSTOMERS

Let's look at a patient who comes in with a real chip on their shoulder. Maybe they're irritated about a legitimate breakdown in one of your systems. Or maybe they're just one of those grumpy sourpusses that are not real fun to be around.

First of all, it's important to differentiate between the two types. Let's say a patient comes in and says, "It's 10 o'clock. Here's my appointment card. I'm here." And their little card says 10 o'clock, but on the chart and on the schedule it says 11 o'clock.

Clearly, someone mistakenly wrote 10 o'clock on the appointment card, and that's a breakdown in our system. It happens. I would be upset, too.

When that happens, I always apologize to the patient.

"I'm so sorry," I say. "First of all, your next cleaning, there's going to be no charge. Second, we're going to see you now. We're not going to make you wait until 11 o'clock."

I don't care what the schedule looks like. We're going to make it work. Now, if you're in a small office, you may have to pull some strings and figure out what you're going to do. But in my office, I can always bring the patient back to a treatment room. I'm going to get their work done, and I'm going get it done in a timely manner.

So, what have I just done? Instead of bundling the patient with a real gripe with a sourpuss who is just griping to gripe, I handled something that was a breakdown in our system.

But let's face it, there are also patients and customers who are buttheads. Every industry has them. They're in education, the automotive industry, health industry, and hospitality industry. They grab, grab, grab, and they stress the team out at every turn. Yet when you walk in the room, they're as sweet as pie.

"Oh, hi, Dr. Bruce, how are you? It's so nice to see you."

And that's tough. It's tough on the team—especially if you push it to the side, ignore and deflect it. And that's what I used to do. I'd look at the team and wink at them as if to say, "All you have to do is be me, team." That response does nothing but put distance between you and your team.

I have learned to handle things differently. Now I look at it as an opportunity. I simply tell the patient, "You know what, Bob? My team loves you. They absolutely love you. But you know what's happened? They tell me that you're always a little bristly when you come in."

And I don't let the patient interrupt.

"The thing is you're never that way with me. But I need to let you know that these people on my team, they're family. That's what they are. They're my family."

And, the patient always apologizes.

I used to wonder what accounted for this invariable turnaround in behavior, but I don't wonder about it so much anymore. I think the reason for their immediate shift in disposition is that usually, one of two things happen when the difficult person exhibits their nasty behavior: 1) they either get their way without any pushback because no one on the receiving end wants to receive any more of their scorn; or 2) the person on the receiving end of their vitriol returns the same exact behavior they're receiving, which only confirms the patient's feeling that their grumpiness is warranted.

But the gentle confrontation with the patient I propose above always ends with an apology from them.

"I am so sorry," they say. "I didn't even realize I was doing it."

This approach to confrontation also becomes an opportunity for you to stand up for your team. And guess what? Your team will return the support by standing up for you all day long, every day.

But you also have to be able to differentiate between this patient and the patient who has a legitimate complaint—the scheduling problem, or maybe the lab didn't get the patient's work here on time.

Let's look at that lab example. Say we put the patient's case in on Tuesday and scheduled a visit with them on Friday afternoon, expecting the case would be here by then. First of all, my team should have already realized that and called the patient to say, "Look, I am so sorry, but the lab will need some extra time"—or whatever the reason is. But act with integrity. Be truthful. Don't blame it on the weather if the weather didn't have anything to do with it.

If someone on your team forgot to send the case to the lab, that's okay. Stuff happens. I'm going to stand by the honest mistake. And we're going to apologize and give the patient and his wife a free cleaning.

Those patients will stay with you for forever, and it's because we're handling the complaint or the objection before it happens. This is what we do throughout our lives, not just in the practice.

And I've told you before, I was terrible at this for the first fifteen years. I was terrible at communicating, and even though I've gotten better, I've still got a lot to learn. And I want to keep learning and keep reading, because people who learn to communicate, to handle objections and complaints before they become objections and complaints, will find an opportunity to improve with every conflict that comes their way.

Chapter 12

CONTINUING EDUCATION

I made the case in the last chapter that legendary leadership doesn't happen without being adept at confrontation management, and this trait does not happen without a commitment to continued education.

Inherent in the phrase "continuing education" is the idea that education comes before *continuing* education, but I'm not talking here about your undergraduate degree and your DDS or DMD or MBA or MSW or whatever degrees—or not even degrees—whatever life experiences have brought you to this exploration of leadership. I'm talking about the life-long process of learning that most of us don't have time to even think about until the formal stuff is done with and the certificates are framed and tacked to our office walls.

I was always a good student, but I can't say that I was driven to be the #1 student in my class. In high school, I ranked thirty-second out of 320, and I made the top ten percent by the skin of my teeth.

In college, I had a great advisor who knew of my dentistry aspirations. He pulled me aside after I made one B in my first semester in freshman biology, and he said, "Well, you're done, Bruce. Sorry about that. In three years, you're going to be in a group of 3,000 students applying to dental school, and they're going to see this B and flip your application in the silver can under their desk."

I'm not sure whether it was a scare tactic or if he was dead serious, but the result was that I didn't make another B. I applied to dental school a year early, with only three years of undergrad under my belt, and, amazingly, was accepted!

I always loved learning. I finished my requirements early, and so I went up to the senior floor to learn about all these other things. I skimmed through the last semester and a half and found that when I got to dental school it was fairly easy.

Two months after I graduated from dental school, I went to Korea and was one half of a two-doctor clinic with 2,500 troops there.

I was there for a year before I came to finish out my military career with Colonel Cryer.

Under Colonel Cryer, we were given the opportunity to take one TDY (temporary duty) trip every year, where we would go somewhere to take a dental course. Well, Colonel Cryer gave me two or three of them every year. He knew I worked extremely hard. When I started with Colonel Cryer, we were the last rated dental unit in the United States Army, and we shot up from the last to the first in one quarter.

Those were my first continuing education opportunities, and there was no one more earnest about milking those opportunities for all they were worth.

And coming back to that military clinic under his astounding leadership—by the way, he was only forty-four years old when I was working for him—and putting my new knowledge to the test was an amazing opportunity for me to do things I had never done before.

There were some really successful people in my class, and before I left the military, I visited a few of the buddies in my class who had opened businesses. I went to their clinics and took notes on legal pads.

I asked them, "What do you love about what you do? What things are spot on? What were some of the problems you faced early on? What things would you do differently?"

When my days in the military came to an end and I opened my own clinic, I looked back to those legal pads and considered all of the pros and cons my former classmates had experienced, and I combined them with my own ideas to set the foundation for the systems I put to work in Granbury, Texas.

I've always been curious. I've always been interested in finding ways to do things efficiently. I hate wasted steps. If there's a better way of doing something, I want to know about it.

And I learned early on not to skimp on the best CE. I went to the top of the mountain in every area I wanted to explore. You find who you think is the best and that's where you go. It might cost more, but it will be best in the long run.

There were experts out there who were already doing the things in dentistry that I wanted to do. When I wanted to learn about dental implants, I went to the best in the business. I went Dr. Carl Misch. Talk about legendary. Misch died in 2017, but from early in life his determination was clear. He was involved in a tragic accident that left him in a burn unit for six months. Before becoming a dentist, he was drafted by the Detroit Tigers and ultimately chose dentistry over baseball, a choice I still can't fathom having to make. The principles and classifications he developed became the origins of modern implant dentistry.

When I wanted to learn about restorative dentistry, I went to Dr. John Kois. The same with business classes. I went to communication workshops with Paul Homoly to learn about communication skills, interpersonal communication, nonverbal communication.

It won't surprise you that I keep coming back to the idea of abundancy and scarcity, because if you're locked in a scarcity mindset, it's difficult to rationalize spending money on the best continuing education opportunities out there. All I can tell you is that getting to a place of real abundance is about more than money. It's about knowledge and education as well.

As soon as I got out of the military, I spent a lot of money I didn't have. I knew it was going to be a long play, not a short play. A marathon, not a sprint.

If I want to learn a new approach or technique, if I'm going to do something off-book, I want—I *need*—to be 100 percent confident in what I'm doing. I need to learn more about it before I do it, I want to be at the highest level of expertise, and that means I need to learn from the best.

Find other ways to save money. Don't skimp on the continuing education.

How many people do you know in all walks of life, in all industries, who roll their eyes and sigh when it comes to the thought of continuing education and professional development? There are countless reasons for this common disappointment about continuing education. Part of the problem is that many workshops and conferences out there are being led by mediocrity. That's not just on the pedestrian talent that's putting on the show, though— that's on us for not doing our homework and going to the top of the mountain to find the pioneers and visionaries, the master teachers and practitioners at the highest levels of the game.

There are no guarantees that any one clinic is going to blow your mind and change your approach to dentistry forever, but you raise the chances of having a great CE experience when you do your homework before signing up for the course. Do your research. Find out who's at the top of the mountain and prepare for the journey.

CONTINUING EDUCATION: A COMMITMENT SPECTRUM

One of the things I observed very soon after starting the Productive Dentist Academy is the wide spectrum of commitment to continuing education. At a typical conference, we might have thirty different clinics represented; so, we'll have maybe 200 people in the room. I think of their levels of participation as falling somewhere on a sort of continuing education commitment spectrum.

CONTINUING EDUCATION COMMITMENT SPECTRUM

THE CARD PUNCHER   THE HALF-HEARTED   COMMITTED LIFELONG LEARNERS

If we apply the 80/20 rule, of the 200 people who come to the course, 80 percent are somewhere between the half-hearted middle of the spectrum and the committed learners on the far right. The other 20 percent are just kind of going through the motions.

THE CARD PUNCHERS

At the far left of the spectrum are the dentists who go to continuing education opportunities just to get their card punched—because the state requires it, because the boss requires it. They sign up, they go, they get their folder, their badge, and maybe even they bring a legal pad to take notes in, but they're not really there. They're working on their phone, they're checking their stocks, they're hiring someone to manage their LinkedIn account, they're looking for their classmates from dental school, and watching the clock move closer to happy hour. They're doing what they have to do so they can get the code at the end of the workshop, so that they can check off the continuing education box.

Maybe they even walk out of the workshop and say, "Man, that was awesome!" But when they go back home, they do nothing. Absolutely nothing. Except they *know* it. They know that they could be better if they did this, and what cognitive dissonance they feel causes internal strife. And I guarantee you that doesn't instill a lot of confidence in the team that sees them come back with a great suntan, but the same old approach to their work.

I can't tell you how many times I've worked with doctors and other clients from this end of the spectrum who say, "Well, you know, I've been to all of these conferences and workshops and I've tried this, I tried that, and you know, it's just not working."

And okay, it's not working. But did you actually do the things that you said you were going to do? Or once you realized it was going to take real work did you decide it wasn't for you?

There's a reason this chapter on continuing education comes after the chapter on abundance vs. scarcity. So often it's the scarcity-constricted mentality that underpins the clinic owner who dismisses CE as a waste of time, or who attends a workshop just to check the CE box.

I've seen it time and time again. We've had people come through the Productive Dentist Academy without ever intending to grow or change. They hire us because they think their team is the problem— they want us to take care of their team, to fix their team.

"You see, Dr. Baird, the problem is my front office assistant …."

Truthfully, most of production problems in a dental practice have less to do with the team than they have to do with the doc who's running the show.

"Oh, well, you know, I just didn't find your stuff to be that helpful." But I look at their practice and they're suffering through all of these issues that are not insurmountable.

"Nothing works … We've always done it this way …"

They're not willing to fully engage in things that deep down they know would make things better. But the reason they have not seen these things through is it takes real effort.

THE HALF-HEARTED

Then there are the folks in the middle who go to the continuing education opportunity with every intention of getting something out of it.

The well-intentioned people in this group might even bring their legal pads and pens. They go to most of the workshops and most of the happy hours down the street, and when they leave the conference and get back home, maybe they even look at their legal pads and type up the notes they took.

They might even recognize the need to send their hygienists to the conference. But of the four hygienists they have on staff, they only send Erica to the course and tell her to take good notes so she can share them with the rest of the team when she returns.

They make a little effort in that first month back, and maybe their production rises. They get excited. They're up $100 an hour, $150 an hour, and they're pumped, but the changes they've made don't become physiologic. They fade into the background, and two months later they're back to where they were before the conference. The energy and excitement diminish, and with the loss of that energy and excitement becomes the loss of commitment.

THE COMMITTED LIFE-LONG LEARNER

I consider myself fortunate that not only have I always been interested in learning, but that I had mentors like Colonel Cryer who introduced continuing education to me as a *reward*—not as a state-required or clinic-required box I had to check off. He was committed to teaching, to growing and learning as a dentist, and he was committed to passing that on to the doctors that worked under him. He presented continuing education to me as a reward for great work, and that approach became a part of my interest in life-long learning.

Even in my early days as a clinic owner in Granbury, Texas, I was committed to CE. We took a team of nineteen people to New York one year for a dental clinic conference. Many of them had never been out of Texas. We went to Hawaii back in the late 80s, and to Cancun other years. This was early on, and I was still years away from being a good boss, but even then, I knew the importance of continuing education, and I carried on Colonel Cryer's approach to thinking about CE as a reward.

And I've seen that same commitment in many dentists who have come to the Productive Dentist Academy. I've seen some people bring their entire team with them. They're 100 percent committed. I've watched them. I've watched how they work with their teams. They're taking notes. When we have breaks in the conference, they have meetings. I often looked at them and wondered if I was ever that committed.

Witnessing that approach to dentistry—especially when I see it in the young clinic owners—gives me a great deal of hope for the future of dentistry.

Keep in mind that commitment to continuing education doesn't mean just accepting everything you hear at a conference or a workshop. But it does require that you listen, that you take notes, that you absorb, that you question, that you consider.

Example: Dr. Edward P. Allen is the best teacher in the world on connective tissue grafting, and after going to his course, I never thought of dentistry the same way. I went home, and I was so excited. I did a couple of tissue grafts, and after my third case I realized I hated doing it. It opened my eyes to the fact my partner who went with me loved doing them! I hated spending forty-five minutes suturing something out. But it's actually amazing stuff, and there are dentists who love it. It just didn't fit with me.

One of the realities of continuing education is that some stuff isn't going to work with your clinic or business. If you're committed to doing good continuing education, there's no doubt that you'll be introduced to brilliant ideas that, for countless reasons, just won't work with your office.

OPEN YOUR MIND TO THE POSSIBILITIES

Sometimes you don't know what you'll get out of a course or a workshop. There's no guarantee that you're going to leave the conference fully charged and ready to set the world on fire, but there are ways to raise the chances that you'll go home with new ideas, new energy, and a renewed commitment to your work. One of the ways, as I mentioned earlier, is to do your research and find the best experts in the country in your field.

Another way is to enter every interaction knowing that you have something to learn from it—whether it's a conventional continuing education course or a new employee who might have a novel way of approaching a problem.

Open your mind to the possibilities even if you find yourself in a workshop on a tired and overworked topic that your summer intern could probably teach. You might hear the presenter turn a sentence in a way that sparks off the creative synapses in your brain and steers you toward another idea that might change the world for you.

If you enter each new experience with an open mind, none of the time you spend learning some new technique or exploring some new process will be squandered.

I ended up realizing that tissue grafting wasn't going to be my thing, but my exploration of it led to my decision to get the Periolase laser, and then I went all out. I mean, I set patients up and I started tracking amazing results. The time I spent trying out the connective tissue grafting absolutely solidified my commitment to the Periolase laser, because when I saw the results, I knew this was something I need to continue doing. And I don't know if I would have come to that realization unless I was committed to giving Dr. Allen's brilliant work a try. I tried it and made a decision that was born of commitment.

Another example was when I first heard John Kois talking about risk factors in dental treatment. Oh, my gosh, it was the catalyst for so many new ideas and provided so much solid rationale for why some things fail and why others succeed. It answered countless questions I hadn't even fully articulated. It made me see how much unnecessary pressure I had been putting on myself over the years. When I heard what John was talking about, it was *new* to me, it was a *new idea* to me, and I knew from that very moment I was never going to think the same way again.

But if I had gone into that session a little foggy from the night before, or I was on my phone checking my email and my Robinhood account, and I wasn't committed to absorbing the material, I would never have been receptive to the message.

Enter every continuing education opportunity with your mind absolutely open to life-changing possibilities. I impress that mindset on everyone on my team and everyone I coach, because I know what happens when you change and when you become seriously committed to whatever it is you want to do. That commitment opens you up to discovering things that you never expected to discover and that you never even saw coming. Your mind starts working differently because you've opened it up to receive what may turn into astonishing ideas. If you're not open to new ideas, I don't know what to tell you. One of the few times I'm absolutely speechless is when I run into someone who isn't open to new ideas.

And so that's what I challenge you to do: to use continuing education opportunities to re-envision your work. Make it your goal to seek out every opportunity to learn. I challenge you not only to listen carefully and take fastidious notes, but to do the deep reflection required to see how this new thought, idea, technique, or practice fits in with your world view. Be open to new ideas!

Chapter 13

EXCELLENCE

The more involved I became in writing this book, the more I realized that I could have made the argument that almost any one of these chapters could probably have been the opening chapter. Without a doubt, "excellence" could have been the opening chapter for this book.

Way back in chapter six I mentioned that perfection is the stuff of dreams. There's no such thing as the perfect practice, no such thing as the perfect team, no such thing as the perfect business. But excellence is still something to shoot for.

Even in my bad-boss days that was my goal. I wanted every facet of the business to be guided by excellence. I wanted to do the best provisional restorations we could possibly do. I wanted to do the best final restorations. From top to bottom, I wanted to take care of patients in an uncommon way, using excellence as my guide. None of that has ever changed for me. I want to go above and beyond the call of duty.

And it wasn't always easy. When we first opened our office down the street from that nuclear power plant, we were seeing 300 new patients a month. And I don't care who you are and how badly you want every patient to have an over-the-top experience; when you have that many new patients, very few of them are going to get an over-the-top experience. There were problems across the board—from hiring issues, to office conflicts, to systems that hadn't been thought out to scale.

We didn't always *achieve* excellence, but there wasn't a day that went by that I didn't strive for it. And I'm working on the assumption that if you've still got this book in your hands, you're with me in this regard.

Over the years, the Productive Dentist Academy has worked with thousands of dentists who want their clinics to see better productivity, and as we steer them to reflect on the current state of affairs in their clinics, we invariably ask them to ponder the question "What is your *why*?"

Why are you doing dentistry? What is your ultimate goal? Why are you in whatever business you're in?

It's a question that some of them have never been asked. For others, the question may come at a time when they're ready to revisit their *why*. Whatever the case, the question inevitably leads them into a conversation about excellence.

Not everyone has excellence as their guiding principle. You'll find people in every industry for whom their work is just a business. They're there to make money, buy their toys, and go home. Don't get me wrong, making money is an important part of the business; I've got a family that I want to take care of, and I've a team of employees who have families that depend on them as well. And I'm the first guy in line to help dentists figure out ways to spend more time with their families.

But the people I worry about are the ones who aren't driven by the goal to take excellent care of their patients and clients.

That's my *why*. I want our work to go above and beyond. I want people to say, "That team at Granbury Dental Center, I mean they are really on top of it. They're great people, they're having fun doing what they do. They like each other. You can just tell they like each other. They help each other out."

How important is it to be guided by excellence? Well, in my opinion, that's where everything needs to start. Excellence *has* to be the driving force of the legendary leader. If you lose sight of that—if you lose sight of the experience and care you're delivering to your patients and clients, you're not allowing your practice or business to flourish.

We're not going to just stick a temporary on there and have it rough. Has it happened before? Yes. But we train away from that. We train excellence, not perfection.

And it's not just about delivering excellent care to your patients. Excellence goes across the board—from hiring people, to training your team, to the labs you contract. If you're not working with a lab that you believe is the best lab in the country, you're not doing everything to foster an environment in which you can flourish.

Every patient who walks in that door deserves an excellent experience.

DO YOU DESERVE A TIP?

I want to share with you something that happened on a trip my wife and I took to the Maldives. If you're in the United States going to the Maldives, it's a long way. It was a 15-hour flight from Dallas and then an eight-hour layover and another five hour-or-so flight down to Mele in the Maldives.

Gorgeous place. Just beautiful. Beautiful fish, beautiful every-thing. I could talk to you all day about that trip, but what I'm mostly interested in talking about here is the notion of customer service. We had the opportunity to fly business class with Qatar on that trip.

I'm a three and a half million-miler on American Airlines, so I've been flying a lot for a long time, but I've never had a flying experience like I did on that flight on Qatar Airlines. And it was funny because they had us up in business class. We were in these Q Suites, and when you get on, of course, they're serving you drinks—champagne or whatever you want—while the rest of the plane is loading, and I remember thinking, "Okay, this is nice. This is awesome."

But before long, I noticed that the attention the flight attendants were paying to us was far more than I expected. Their people came around and checked in on us through the entire flight.

"Is there anything else that I can do to make you more comfortable?"

"How are you enjoying the flight so far?"

"Do you have any questions about the menu?"

"Would you like another drink, sir?"

"Eye mask? Slippers? A bottle of water? A smoothie?"

A smoothie. They made smoothies for us. And just on and on and on. There was no end to it.

And this was not just one person on the plane, and it wasn't just those of us in business class. This was everybody. Every time I turned around, there was someone on their team asking if anyone needed anything. Toothbrushes, toothpaste, toothpicks, lotion, cologne—you name it.

And at the end of the trip Cynthia, my wife, turned to me and said, "Should we tip them?"

What struck me first, of course, was the question, "Are we supposed to tip them?" But what really hit me was that after flying more than three and a half million miles and never tipping a flight attendant, I wasn't absolutely certain how to respond. And that's what absolutely hit me right between the eyes.

If Cynthia had asked me during any one of three and a half million miles I had flown on, if we were supposed to tip the flight attendants, I wouldn't have had to think about it. Of course, we don't tip flight attendants.

But I said, "I don't know."

I had to actually think about the answer.

That's the extent to which they provided uncommon service to us.

We were both so impressed by this customer service that it made a long lasting impression on us! I am always looking for connections between dentistry and other industries. Isn't this the question we all want our patients, customers, and clients to be asking themselves after an experience with us?

What kind of service are we providing in our dental practice? Is that the way our patients feel about our practice? Do we provide the kind of service that would prompt our patients to wonder if they should give us a tip?

I started thinking about how we could do this in our practices—how we could provide that kind of uncommon excellence to our patients. From the doctors, to the leadership, to the hygienists, to the front office—how do we present ourselves? Do you think about this in your business?

What is it that helps you shift from being a *good* practice to being a *great* practice to being a *sought-after* practice? The sought-after practice is the one whose entire team is on the same page. And the page the sought-after team is always on is the page about going that extra mile.

I'm convinced that the shift to a sought-after team begins with the question, *What is your why?* And there are dozens of ways to ask the question: What are you here for? What is your motivation? What is your ultimate goal?

No matter how you frame the question, the bottom line has to be that you're here to serve your patients, your clients, your customers. People are starving for excellence. They're starving for customer service. And you're there to give them the best service possible. The rest will take care of itself.

There's a reason why Qatar is ranked the number one airline in the world, and with that same approach to customer service, there's no reason why you can't be the number one dental practice or the number one business in the world.

ACKNOWLEDGMENTS

I would like to thank all of my dental mentors. The late Pete Dawson who always encouraged me toward excellence. The late Dr. Carl Misch and Dr. Hilt Tatum who taught me the why about implant dentistry. My friend, Dr. John Kois, who gave me the freedom to evaluate patients' risk factors as a cause of dental problems. I must also acknowledge Dr. Paul Homoly for among other things, his inspiring work in communication. Also, Mr. Imtiaz Manji who sharpened my business mind over the years. Dr. Mark Morin, who trailblazed digital dentistry to the mainstream and has continued to be a soundboard for my crazy business ideas.

My partner over the last fifteen years in my dental practice, Dr. Jeff Buske, a ravenous seeker of dental truth who always challenges me to learn. I would like to say a special thanks to Dr. Victoria Peterson who has helped shape the Productive Dentist Academy into a world-class coaching and marketing company known throughout the world, as well as Dr. David Porritt and Mr. Mike Brown who guided Comprehensive Finance into an industry leading FinTech company. Finally, I have to thank Dr. Herb Salisbury and Dr. Ernest Robertson for always being there for me through thick and thin.

I would like to thank my friends who have come through the Productive Dentist Academy and the current group of innovators in dentistry: the likes of Dr. Mark Costes, Dr. John Meis, Dr. Frank Spear, Mr. Gary Takacs, Dr. Howard Farran, Dr. David Hornbrook, to name a few. I would also like to thank Mr. Steve Cain from Cain Watters & Associates for taking amazing care of me over the years. My journey through dentistry over the last forty years would have been much more difficult without the help of the world-class Root Dental Lab and their founder, the late Dan Root. I must also acknowledge J.C. Cramer, Rick Maynord, Brian Ripley, and Randy Root, the best lab guys in the world. I would like to thank all of my past employees who made me the leader I am today.

And I would be remiss if I didn't acknowledge my father who taught me the value of hard work and perseverance; my mother who gave me my sense of humor and the ability to see love in anyone. They both left this life too soon. I have to thank my beautiful daughters who taught me to speak a different language and helped me see the good in people. And finally, my wife, Cynthia, who continues every day to support my goal to make a difference!

ABOUT THE AUTHOR

Dr. Bruce B. Baird is a 1980 graduate of the University of Texas Health Science Dental School in San Antonio. After graduation, he spent four years in the United States Army in Korea and at Ft. Sam Houston in San Antonio. After leaving the service, he built his dental practice from scratch in the small town of Granbury, Texas. Over the next thirty-six years, he grew the practice into a multi-doctor business with revenue over five million dollars in 2019.

Dr. Baird has lectured across the United States and internationally for over thirty years. His topics include leadership, cosmetic dentistry, dental implants, communication skills, and the business of dentistry. He taught at the Implant preceptorship at the University of Texas Health Science Center Dental School in San Antonio and to the seniors at Baylor Dental School.

Dr. Baird founded Productive Dentist Academy in 2004, which has grown into a world class organization with doctors from all fifty states and nineteen countries attending various workshops. With his partner, Dr. Victoria Peterson, they have grown the company to over thirty employees, providing seminars, coaching, and marketing to thousands of dentists across North America.

In 2011, Dr. Baird founded Comprehensive Finance Inc. (CFI), a company that helps businesses across the United States do their own in-house financing. The company has helped originate over 300 million dollars in financing across multiple industries, and rapidly became one of the largest financial tech companies in healthcare. CFI was sold in June of 2021 to AKKR, one of the largest private equity firms in the world. Dr. Baird has continued with the company as a key opinion leader and investor.

Dr. Baird is a coach, mentor, podcaster, international lecturer, keynote speaker, author, and serial entrepreneur. He has successfully started multiple profitable businesses across diverse industries. He is known for his relatable and down-to-earth speaking style.